SECRETS OF THE
MASTERS

31 Wealth-Building Strategies from the World's Most Successful Investors

The Oxford Club

TABLE OF CONTENTS

INTRODUCTION

A Letter from *The Oxford Club*

Dear Fellow Investor,

The book you're holding, *Secrets of the Masters*, contains the greatest moneymaking insights of the top 1% of the world's investors.

People like Bill Gross, Jeremy Grantham, Jim Rogers – men whose investing strategies and techniques have propelled their clients' net worth, as well as their own, to truly dizzying heights.

More importantly for you, the secrets of these master investors are just as profitable today as they've ever been. And you have them at the tips of your fingers, courtesy of the research team at *The Oxford Club*...

Now, it's up to you to dig in and decide which you'll put to work in your own portfolio... and when. Will it be...

- Using **Chris Weber's** "conservative" *Max Yield Strategy*, to earn more than 3,100% in cash...
- Following **David Ricardo's** *One Simple Rule of Investing*, the same one that helped one 14-year old boy earn his own $52 million fortune...
- Taking advantage of **Mark Cook's** *Big Secret* to turn every <u>$10,000 you invest into $56,300</u>.
- Or one of the other 28 secrets of the masters?

But that's not all you'll take away from *Secrets*. You'll also learn how to safely manage risk, consistently buy low and sell high, find the types of companies that double and triple in value, and – in the end – create long-lasting wealth.

With that, I take pride in presenting to you: *Secrets of the Masters*. Now it's your turn to begin investing like the world's wealthiest 1%.

Good investing,

Julia Guth
Executive Director and Publisher
The Oxford Club

JEREMY GRANTHAM
How To Make Money That Grows On Trees

Trees? As an investment? You've probably never considered it. But you ought to...

Historically, timber has performed incredibly well. According to legendary investor **Jeremy Grantham**, timber prices have beaten inflation by 3.3% a year over the last century.

Add in 6% a year in income (from cutting trees), and 2.5% a year in inflation, and you've got returns of nearly 12% a year in timber... that beats the return on stocks! Even better, the returns on timber have been less volatile than the stock market. Investing in timberland stacks up very well versus stocks.

Here are some of the reasons you might consider adding a timber investment or two to your portfolio. Then, we'll share with you the easiest way to invest in timber. It's simple – you buy a stock on the NYSE!

Why Invest in Timber?

In a nutshell:

- **Timber beats stocks**. Managed timber (as the professional investors call it), has actually beaten the stock market – with less risk – over the long run. Historically, investments in timberland have provided total real returns (net of inflation) of 6-10%, and nominal returns of 9-15% according to Hancock Timber Resource Group.

- **Timber is uncorrelated to stocks**. Trees don't know

about the war in Iraq and Afghanistan or a bear market in stocks. While stocks couldn't keep up with inflation in the 1970s, timberland never had a losing year! Trees just keep growing year after year. So timber is an excellent way to balance your portfolio as its value rises even when stocks are falling.

- **Timberland is relatively cheap**. Lumber is almost half the price it was 5 years ago. And as many investment gurus will say "buy low, sell high" – and that is good news for us since timberland prices correlate with lumber, and are relatively cheap.

- **The price of timber has consistently beaten inflation**. Timber is thought of as a good inflation hedge, and Jeremy Grantham's numbers – timber prices rising at 3.3% above the rate of inflation over the past century – show that to be true.

The Demand for Timber Isn't Going Away

Oxford Club Senior Analyst, Louis Basenese recently spent some time driving around the Olympic peninsula in Washington state with a forestry consultant, looking at more timberland to potentially invest in. And it only confirmed his belief that timber is a great investment right now:

> "*The head of the timber company I met with in Washington told me that **every American 'consumes' a 100-foot tree... every year**. He pointed out that I was taking notes on paper (from a tree), sitting at a conference table made of wood, in a wooden chair, in a room with wood trim all around, in a one story office that was likely framed with, well, wood.*"

Are there alternative materials other than wood that could have been used? Sure. But the use of wood doesn't appear to be shrinking. Don't be alarmed by this if you're considering investing in timberland... thinking that timber companies are cutting down forests with abandon... Forest science is highly advanced. Louis stood among 36-year-old Douglas fir trees in Washington state that will likely be cut in the next few years. When cut, they'll be in excess of 100 feet tall. And yet, this will be the fourth time this "stand" (as they call it) has been "harvested."

Instead of chopping down a forest and moving on, it is in the best interest of timberland companies to think in the very long term, and harvest in a sustainable way. In essence, in Washington, they'll cut and replant roughly 1/40th of their forest every year.

Some folks who don't understand how the world works want to shut down timber operations in the U.S. There are timber operations in emerging market countries: secretive, unscrupulous operators slashing down rainforests in such a way that those rainforests will be gone forever. Wouldn't you rather have your wood products coming from regulated, publicly traded U.S. timber companies that are accountable, and that practice "sustainable" growth?

The Easiest Way To Invest in Timber

The timberland consultant Lou met in the Washington woods worked at **Rayonier** (NYSE: RYN) for years. Rayonier is a REIT and is among the largest direct timber plays you can buy. The company knows timber, and is a shrewd manager of its 2.5 million-plus acres of quality land.

That's just one reason Rayonier's risen 79.66% in the past year and a half (see chart on following page. Meanwhile, the S&P is up just 40% over the same period).

The company traditionally pays dividends in the 4-5% range. And it's relatively cheap, with timber assets valued at

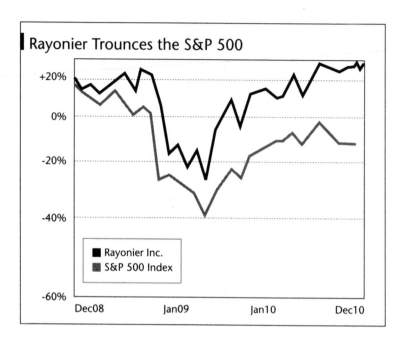

Rayonier Trounces the S&P 500

only $800 to $1,500 per acre (depending on how you crunch your numbers). Rayonier's still an excellent way to play the bull market in natural resource commodities that just keeps building up steam.

Timber is something you should consider putting in your portfolio. It's beaten stocks, with less volatility. It's uncorrelated to the stock market. You get paid high dividends. And you own millions of acres of exceptional real estate in the U.S. for around $1,000 an acre.

DAVID RICARDO
One Simple Rule Of Investing That's Worth $52 Million

Financial forecasts are worthless. That's a bold statement, perhaps. But the reality is nobody knows if the Nasdaq will be at 500 or 5,000. And nobody knows if the economy will be booming or in recession, or if inflation will be 5% or -5%. Economists don't make forecasts because they believe they know the future. They simply make them because that's what they're paid to do...

Dr. Mark Skousen, Advisory Panelist of *The Oxford Club* – and an economist himself – wrote *The Making of Modern Economics: The Lives and Ideas of the Great Thinkers* and included three economists in particular who both changed economic history and made millions speculating.

All have compelling stories... but the first one made his fortune by following one simple rule.

The Man Who Discovered the Most Important Rule of Investing

David Ricardo (1772-1823) is credited with discovering a number of economic truths. Some consider him the most important economic thinker since Adam Smith. Yet, what most people don't know is that he is credited with discovering the most important rule of investing and speculating. His simple investing rule made him extraordinarily rich – and it can help you as well. (More on that in a moment.)

For now, just know that **by understanding Ricardo's key principles and investing based on them, you will undoubtedly improve your investing success** as well. Ricardo promoted free trade, hard money, the laws of comparative advantage, and more economic principles that are widely accepted today. (Although in some cases, Ricardo's ideas seemed outrageous at the time).

Two Historic Policy Changes That Led to The Industrial Revolution

First, as a strong advocate of "Sound Money," Ricardo persuaded the British parliament to establish a strict anti-inflation monetary standard (which it did pass, called the Peel Act). This is the same goal the world's central bankers have today.

And second, on the matter of free trade, Ricardo sharply criticized England's high tariffs on agricultural goods. This led to a repeal of the "Corn Laws," and ultimately led to freer trade in the world. In another part of his "Corn Laws" critique, he also defined the "Law of Diminishing Returns," an economic concept that stands to this day.

These two historic policy changes (sound money and lower costs of trade) led us into the Industrial Revolution and led England to become the "workshop of the world," importing food and exporting all kinds of clothing and manufactured goods.

A Remarkable Investing Career... Based On One Simple Rule for Investing

Ricardo didn't just crunch numbers. He also loved to be a part of "the game." His father was a stockbroker and by age 14, Ricardo worked with his father at the London Stock Exchange. In time, Ricardo was trading for his own account and making a market as well (similar to a floor trader today).

Ricardo's investing career made a huge leap forward when he began bidding as a loan contractor for the government. Ricardo's firm held its own, competing with such big names as the Barings and the Rothschilds. The last – and biggest – loan of the Battle of Waterloo was raised on June 14, 1815.

According to Skousen's book:

> "*The price of the bonds was extremely depressed because of the size of the loan and the uncertainty of the outcome of the war. There were four bidders for the loan contract, but Ricardo's firm won.*

> "*Ricardo bravely held onto his position in the deeply depressed bonds, his biggest gamble ever. Other more timid investors sold early, before the Battle of Waterloo, but not Ricardo. He held on after the shocking news arrived that Wellington had won the battle against Napoleon. The government consols (bonds) skyrocketed and Ricardo became an instant millionaire. The Sunday Times reported in Ricardo's obituary a popular rumor that during the Battle of Waterloo Ricardo had 'netted upwards of a million sterling.'*"

Ricardo's $52 Million Payoff... And The Golden Rule That Made It Possible

A million sterling in 1815 translates into about $52 million in today's dollars. Once Ricardo gained his fortune, he lost interest in the London Stock Exchange. He became a "country gentleman" – living the good life and writing his ideas about economics in *On the Principles of Political Economy and Taxation*, his economics masterwork, published in 1817.

In addition to the economic principles he created, he also defined and explained the "Law of Comparative Advantage," arguably one of the greatest laws in economics. This law proves how free trade benefits both nations, and that it pays for each nation and each individual to specialize, as it increases total output.

And possibly Ricardo's greatest contribution to the investing world is what we at *The Oxford Club* refer to as "**The Golden Rule Of Investing.**" Ricardo is credited as the first to say, "Cut short your losses and let your profits run on." Following this invaluable advice may be the single best thing you can do to improve your investing results – regardless of how you invest.

Cut your losers short and let your winners ride. That's about all you need to know. Thanks, David Ricardo.

JOHN TEMPLETON
The Five-Step Plan For Financial Independence

In 2005, billionaire mutual fund magnate John Templeton appeared on video at the London Money Show. He was 93 years old at the time, but looked very alert. And although he spent more time on his religious and charitable work, he remained an avid investor until his death in July of 2008.

The crowd was shocked by his answers to a series of questions…

Terrorism? "Not a serious threat… it's unimportant."

Wall Street scandals and Sarbanes-Oxley? "Not a major problem for business."

Inflation? "Not to worry." (And gold? "Not a bull market!")

Future dollar crisis? "No way."

Economic growth? "I see no interruption in our standard of living, which could be 100 times better by the end of this century."

The only concern he expressed was about "creeping socialism" and government regulation of business around the world.

John Templeton was an incurable optimist – 9/11, the burgeoning deficits, and the deflation or inflation scares did not deter him from a rosy outlook.

Still, we live in a series of short-term events that make up the long term. And it's hard to ignore the recent problems we've faced as investors: A stock market that has seen one of the worst recessions since the Great Depression , record trade and spending deficits, Fed rates stuck at extremely low levels, plus terrorist attacks and natural disasters. When will the sun come out again on Wall Street?

While we wait patiently, here's what John Templeton can teach us…

1. Take calculated risks. Templeton started off by taking significant risks in his business and investments. He was a serious poker player in college, and in 1939, he borrowed $10,000 from his boss to bet on 100 stocks listed on the NYSE selling for under a buck. A high percentage of these companies were close to bankruptcy, but Templeton reasoned that they would recover during a wartime economy. (It pays to have a correct "macro" view of the world.) In four years, he sold all the stocks, paid off the debt, and pocketed $40,000 in profit. He was on his way to success.

2. Save, don't spend. Templeton started out poor, but through the principles of thrift and hard work, he was able to get ahead. When he married, he and his wife set a goal of saving 50% of their income. He avoided consumer debt – in fact, he bought his first home with cash. He carried his "cheap" approach into later life.

He always worked hard, putting in 60 hours a week. He would agree with J. Paul Getty, whose motto was, "Make your money first… then think about spending it."

3. Shop for value investments. Templeton followed the fundamental "bargain-hunting" approach to investing. "The long-range view requires patience." His Templeton Growth Fund, which he ran for 50 years before turning it over to the Franklin Group, held stocks for an average six to seven years. He always searched for companies around the world that offered low prices and an excellent long-term outlook. "It's not easy," he stated, "but if you're going to buy the best bargains, look in more than one industry, and look in more than one nation."

Under Templeton's managing skills, the Templeton Growth Fund <u>averaged a 14% annualized return over 50 years</u>, far out-performing the stock market indexes.

Templeton rejected the "technical" method of trading stocks. "You must be a fundamentalist to be really successful in the market," he said. The best technicians make the most profitable trades in companies with sound fundamentals in sales and earnings.

4. Take advantage of international free markets. Templeton believed a "free enterprise" approach is mandatory when investing overseas. "Avoid investing in those countries with a high level of socialism or government regulation of business," he said. "Business growth depends on a strong free-enterprise system." He was a follower of free-market economists Ludwig von Mises, Friedrich Hayek and Milton Friedman. "Governments should stop interfering with what people want to do."

Templeton took a 'round-the-world tour in 1936, and he was struck by the poverty in India and Hong Kong. When he returned 40 years later, he noted a sharp contrast. "The standard of living in Hong Kong has multiplied more than tenfold in 40 years," he said, "while the standard of living in Calcutta has improved hardly at all. The major difference is between free enterprise and socialism. The Indian government regulates nearly everything, so there's very little progress; whereas in Hong Kong, the government keeps its hands off."

Note: Since Templeton wrote this in 1976, things are changing rapidly. India, for example, is now pursuing market-friendly policies.

5. Minimize your taxes. In the 1960s, Templeton made a

controversial decision. He decided to renounce his U.S. citizenship and move to the Bahamas, where there is no income tax or investment tax. He became a British citizen, and a Bahamian citizen, and lived tax-free (the Bahamas gets its revenue from high import duties and corporate/trust fees).

Interestingly, his investment record improved markedly after he stopped worrying about the tax consequences of his investment decisions. As a result of tax-free compounding, Templeton was worth several billion dollars, and was one of the wealthiest men in the world.

However, Templeton did not recommend that American investors follow his lead and switch allegiance to a tax haven such as the Bahamas (it's almost impossible for an American to become a Bahamian citizen today). But Templeton strongly recommended that you should take full advantage of tax-deferral vehicles, such as a corporate pension plan or an IRA, and incorporate your business.

RICHARD RUSSELL
How To Use the Reliable "Dow Theory" To Assess Stocks

"I've never seen anything like it... it's the most flagrant divergence and series of non-confirmations in the history of the U.S. stock market." ~ **RICHARD RUSSELL**

Richard Russell looks at the stock market all day, every day... Right now, he doesn't like what he's sees. Russell has been writing *Dow Theory Letters*, one of the oldest and most widely recognized newsletters in the financial world, for more than 50 years. He is well known for making great stock market calls like the one he made in 1974...

In December of 1974, the Dow Industrial Average was down 35% for the year. Stocks had basically done nothing for 12 years. People had lost money in stocks for so long that they couldn't stand the thought of buying them. Wall Street was in despair. That's when Russell encouraged his subscribers to buy. Russell got it right. The Dow rallied 75% over the next 18 months.

So how did he do it?

The Oldest Stock Market Indicator Around

Richard Russell uses an indicator called "Dow Theory" to help him make market calls like his 1974 "call to buy." We'll look at "Dow Theory" today, and we'll see why it says you should be very careful about buying stocks right now. *Charles Dow* developed "Dow Theory" in the late 1800s in his publication, *The Wall Street Journal*. He wanted to find a way to predict the big trends in the stock market.

Dow developed two market indexes, the **Dow Industrials** and the **Dow Rails** (now **Dow Transports**). He figured if both industrial stocks (representing production) and transport stocks (representing distribution) were moving up, then the two indexes were in "agreement," meaning the stock market and economy were in good shape.

Dow called this agreement between the two averages a "confirmation." Dow also considered the market to be ready for a "sell-off " when one of the indexes rose to a new high while the second index lagged behind. As Dow's work became the basis for modern technical analysis, many of his students used his theory to make fortunes in the stock market.

Russell also pointed out that the essence of "Dow Theory" is *values*. Charles Dow advocated buying stocks when you can get a great deal for your money, when stocks are cheap. For example, **Dow liked to buy stocks when the overall market had a Price-to-Earnings ratio of 8**.

Buy When They're Cheap; Sell When They're Expensive

Dow also advocated selling stocks when they got expensive. The current volatile market is making Richard Russell cautious right now. He wants his subscribers to keep their stock market exposure light... and keep plenty of their assets in cash and gold. Just like any other stock market tool, the "Dow Theory" shouldn't be used alone to help you make your investment decisions – but history has proved it's a valuable guide to size up the big picture. Right now, "Dow Theory" says, "be careful." Wall Street legends like Richard Russell are heeding its warning. You should, too.

JESSE LIVERMORE
"Be Right, Sit Tight"... And Maximize Your Profits From the Next Bull Run

"Millions come easier to a trader after he knows how to trade than hundreds did in the days of his ignorance." ~ LEGENDARY TRADER **JESSE LIVERMORE** IN THE 1923 TRADING CLASSIC, REMINISCENCES OF A STOCK OPERATOR

Stocks are still expensive, but you should get ready for another bull run, because you never know when the next one will begin.

Yeah, we might be in the middle of a long-term secular bear market that started with the mortgage crisis in 2007, but bull rallies can and should merit our attention when they happen.

So what do you do in a bull market? How do you trade it? Should you sell what you've got once your stocks are up a certain percentage? Or should you try to ride it for a few more points?

But then what? What's the right thing to do, and when should you do it? We get asked these questions every time the market is in an upward trend. And the best answer we can give at times like that is: *"It's a bull market!"*

Now, this answer may seem like not enough information at first. But the following excerpt from **Jesse Livermore's** *Reminiscences of a Stock Operator* – the most sought-after and best-selling book ever written on the stock market – should make this answer crystal clear. In *Reminiscences of a Stock Operator*, Livermore writes:

The Wisdom of Old Turkey

"*The customers used to go into Old Turkey (a nickname, of course) and tell him what some friend of a friend had advised them to do in a certain stock. But whether the tip they had was to buy or sell, the old chap's answer was always the same.*

"*The customer would finish the tale of his perplexity and then ask: 'What do you think I ought to do?' "Old Turkey would cock his head to one side, contemplate his fellow customer with a fatherly smile, and finally he would say very impressively, 'You know, it's a bull market!'*

"*Time and again I heard him say, 'Well, this is a bull market, you know!' as though he were giving to you a priceless talisman wrapped up in a million-dollar accident-insurance policy. And of course I did not get his meaning...*

"*I think it was a long step forward in my trading education when I realized at last that when Old Turkey kept on telling the other customers, 'Well you know this is a bull market!' he really meant to tell them that the big money was not in the individual fluctuations but in the main movements – that is... in sizing up the entire market and its trend.*

"*After spending many years in Wall Street and after making and losing millions of dollars, I want to tell you this: It was never my thinking that made the big money for me. It always was my sitting.*

"*... Men who can both be right and sit tight are*

uncommon. I found it one of the hardest things to learn. But it is only after a stock operator has firmly grasped this that he can make big money. It is literally true that millions come easier to a trader after he knows how to trade than hundreds did in the days of his ignorance... Old Turkey was dead right in doing and saying what he did. He had not only the courage of his convictions, but the intelligent patience to sit tight.

"... Nobody can catch all the fluctuations. In a bull market your goal is to buy and hold until you believe that the bull market is near its end. To do this, you must study general conditions and not tips or special factors affecting individual stocks. You have to use your brains and your vision to do this; otherwise my advice would be as idiotic as to tell you to buy cheap and sell dear."

Taking Old Turkey's Advice Today

What Livermore is saying with his story about Old Turkey is that you can worry about valuations, trade deficits, corporate profits, unemployment, or whatever you want. There are plenty of excuses not to become involved in a bull market. But none of them can overcome the fact that a **bull market's a bull market – and stocks rise with the market.**

The point is to stay in as long as possible. But how do you know when the bull market will end? Who knows?

As Jim Rogers tells us: "The market will rise higher than (we) think is possible." Heck, it already has, many times before.

However, there is a general way to determine that a bull

market has ended. To put a number on it, we'd say a 9% fall in the overall market would cause us to start selling significantly. We like to study the very long-term trends.

We'd consider a bull market to be over when the overall market closes below its 45-week moving average.

JIM ROGERS
Where To Go When Inflation Strikes

"When things go wrong, governments have always printed money, at least in the last few decades," stated investment legend Jim Rogers in a recent interview with Ron Hera of Hera Research, LLC. "Printing money has always led to inflation, eventually. That's all they know and they will do it again. There will be times, obviously, when the printing presses slow down or even stop but when things get bad again, they start over, and that's all they know."

Inflation is a word that investors hate to hear, and Jim Rogers is no stranger to the downside that inflation can wreak on portfolios.

Rogers earned degrees from Yale and Oxford Universities, where he studied politics, philosophy and economics. He co-founded the Quantum Fund in 1970, which gained 4200% over a 10-year period, during which the S&P advanced approximately 47%.

After retiring at age 37, he managed his own portfolio while serving as a guest professor of finance at the Columbia University Graduate School of Business, the moderator of WCBS' "The Dreyfus Roundtable" and host of the Financial News Network's (FNN) "The Profit Motive with Jim Rogers."

So when a man with as much experience as Jim Rogers speaks, we listen…

Rogers suggests that China and other global economies should increase interest rates to contain a surge in inflation. He believes that everyone should be raising interest rates, and thinks they are too low worldwide.

China's central bank hasn't increased rates since November 2007. In the U.S., the Federal Reserve recently left the overnight interbank lending rate target in a range of zero to 0.25 percent, where it's been since December 2008. And the European Central Bank has kept its key interest rate at a record low of 1 percent.

Policy makers in Malaysia, South Korea, Taiwan and Thailand have increased the cost of borrowing at least once this year, while India has boosted rates four times in five months.

"The global economy is at risk of prolonging a recession, as U.S. home sales are still down and Japan's export growth is still slow," stated Rogers.

"We never got out of the first recession," Rogers said. "If the U.S. and Europe continue to slow down, that's going to affect everyone. The Chinese economy is 1/10 of the U.S. and Europe and India is a quarter of China; they can't bail us out." Unfortunately, this scenario usually leads governments to print more money and drive up inflation as they try to stimulate their economies.

How to Protect Yourself from Inflation

Rogers feels that the best way to protect your wealth from inflation is to own commodities. "Throughout history, the way you defend yourself when currencies are being debased is that you own real goods. Whether that's silver or cotton or natural gas or whatever it happens to be, you own something that's a real good. As the value of money is debased, some things will maintain their value and some will even increase."

Protect yourself from inflation. The Fed controls the money-printing press. You need to defend yourself, and commodities are one of the best fortresses you have.

Rogers notes that gold has historically been a good way to preserve wealth, though he also points out that it isn't the only one. "I own gold. Gold is making all-time highs. It certainly has been a way to preserve wealth in the last decade. Whether there are better things in the next decade or not – and I suspect that there will be better things – I do own gold."

Rogers believes that silver is a great commodity that is on the bargain rack right now, and as such, is a great alternative to gold. "Silver is about 70% below its all-time high. Gold is making all-time highs. Often, one is better off investing in things that are down 70%, rather than things that are making all-time highs."

Investors don't have to sit on the sidelines and watch their money devalue from inflation. "Commodities will go above their old high[s] sometime in the next decade even if they only grow 5 to 6 percent annually," said Rogers. Consider the attractive opportunities that exist in commodities as a way to beat inflation.

PAUL TUDOR JONES
When *Not* To Listen To Your Broker

The most successful investors in the world know there are times *not* to be fully invested. **Paul Tudor Jones** is one of the most successful investors of all time. For example, $10,000 invested with him 25 years ago would be worth $1.4 million today. And his investment philosophy is simple, as summed up in an article from *Bloomberg Markets* magazine:

> "*If you don't see anything, you don't trade... You take risk only when you see an opportunity.*"

Don't Fall Prey to the Sales Pitch

Mutual funds and financial planners prey on your need to "put your money to work." In general, the Templeton Group is well-respected as exceptional value investors in foreign stock markets in general and in emerging markets in particular.

But an editorial in the *Financial Times*, penned by the Chief Investment Officer of the Templeton funds group in the *Financial Times*, was a good reminder that the Templeton group, like all mutual fund companies, is in the business to sell funds to make a profit. (Templeton in particular, as part of a publicly traded company, has an even stronger incentive.)

The editorial's mission was to remind us to diversify globally. The article included profoundly bland quotes like: "*It is time to adopt a global approach... and invest wherever and whenever valuations are the most favorable.*" And: "*A global approach broadens investors' choices, which allows them to ride valuation waves between emerging and developed countries.*"

You can try to "ride valuation waves" but what you'll find — and this is brutally true right now — is that if the U.S. stock market falls, markets will fall from Germany to Hong Kong.

You can count on it – "riding valuation waves" or not. Statistically speaking, the world's stock markets are more correlated than they ever have been.

But we feel that the late Sir John Templeton, founder of the Templeton Group, might even have been *insulted* by this article. If Sir John Templeton were holding the reigns right now, he might have felt such an article to be disingenuous, promoting this stuff at this moment. Had he written an editorial, chances are he would likely be looking for investments outside of the stock market. The reason? Today, there is barely a stock market in the world that constitutes "a real bargain" under Templeton's principles.

You Don't Have To Be Fully Invested All the Time

In the mutual fund industry, the business only grows if the assets under management grow. In plain English, that means they want your money. We at *The Oxford Club* have a great luxury – the ability to be totally truthful... we aren't trying to get you to invest more money. And that's why at times we'll be telling you: **This is not a good time to be fully invested**.

Don't feel crazy for holding some money in the bank rather than "putting it to work" all the time. Instead, sleep more comfortably at night. Cash and other investments outside the stock market will likely be safer and better diversification than international stocks.

JACK SCHWAGER AND MARK COOK:

Supercharge Your Trading With This "Secret System" In Just Minutes a Day

As you will read in popular author **Jack Schwager's** excellent investing book, *Stock Market Wizards*, Mark Cook knows how to make *lots* of money in the stock market...

In a trading contest in 1992, his return was 563%... and in the next contest, his return was 322%. It was no fluke... since then, his annual returns have ranged from 30% to 1,422%. This lesson is all about **Mark Cook's Big Secret**. And once you understand what this big secret is (and put it to work in your investing) it may be the key to making the same kinds of triple- and quadruple-digit returns that Mark has made with startling consistency through the years.

First, a little background... Let's start at the point when Mark was hitting rock bottom, very early in his career, when he was really just a kid without a clue...

A Twenty-Something Farmer in Hock for a Half-Million

When Mark started out as a 20-year-old, he ran into trouble, and quickly. Here's a portion of a conversation taken from Schwager's book in which the young Mark Cook told his mother about his predicament.

> *"Mom, I lost $100,000 of your money."*
> *"How much did YOU lose Mark?"*
> *"I lost half a million dollars."*
> *"But you don't have half a million dollars."*

"I know, Mom."
"Besides losing all this money, what else is wrong?"
"That's it, Mom."
"Oh is that all! I thought you had cancer... How long until you make it back?"

Mark didn't give up. After years of studying the market, filling volumes of market diaries, and studiously recording and analyzing every trade he made, his trading became consistently profitable. Five years later, he sat his parents down again...

"What's the bad news this time?"
"I have an income tax problem... (these new investments are now) worth $750,000."
"How much did you invest?"
"Fifty-five thousand dollars"
"Gosh, take it."
"No, they (the investments) are going up more tomorrow."

Mark cashed out the next day with a $1.4 million profit. Things had turned around completely for him.

How He Turned It All Around

It didn't happen overnight; it happened over time. All those notes he took on his trading allowed him to consistently tweak and improve on what he had been doing. Years of little improvements turned into a big improvement in results. *Mark Cook documents all his trading activity. And in order for you to get better, you should do the same.* That is his "big secret."

If you want to have a chance at being like Mark Cook, with many years of extraordinary returns, then you need to start acting like him... at least in this way. **You need to document:**

- Your reasons for getting into a trade

- Your reasons you sold

- Did you follow your rules?

- What you might have done differently for this trade to have worked out better

Only if you do this self-analysis for every investment you make will you get better. You'll start to see your recurrent mistakes, and your results will improve. It's almost guaranteed. If you don't do this, chances are you'll make the same investment mistakes again and again... for the rest of your life.

There are other questions you should know about yourself and your investing, before you make another investment...

- **What are your objectives?** Are you looking to make 4%, 40%, or 400%? If you need safe, stable income from your investments, for example, then you shouldn't be trading options. You can trade options if you decide to... but you must recognize that it is not part of your core objective.

- **What's your timeframe for an investment?** Three days, three months, or three years?

- **How much time per week can you devote to your investments?** If it's an hour or less, then you shouldn't be trading on a short-term basis. Your timeframe should likely be a year or longer.

- **What are you going to trade?** Your investment style needs to fit with your personality.

- **What's your investment edge?** To really succeed, you need to define this... If you don't have an edge, then how can you really expect to outperform the other guy?

- **What are your rules?** Do you use a 25% trailing stop or have no more than 2% at risk? Do you only buy stocks that have positive earnings? Or that are below a P/E of 15?

- **What is the worst possible case, and can you deal**

with that? Can you handle that stock crashing? Or in Mark Cook's case, that naked option that cost him a half-million dollars?

What is truly the worst case? If you seriously try to sit down and write the answers out to all of these, chances are you will discover that you have a lot of problems in your existing investments. You may say, "Why the heck did I buy that?

CRUNCHING THE NUMBERS YOURSELF

People often ask us what software programs we use to crunch numbers... we've used all the expensive programs in the past and the popular technical-analysis software programs MetaStock and TradeStation that can be hundreds of dollars a month. While they're excellent, unless you're a big institution or a day-trading technical analyst, you don't need them.

You can do everything you need with Microsoft Excel and a super cheap but powerful companion program called XLQ. XLQ pumps tons of information on stocks into Excel in a way that is easy to manipulate. Your analysis is really only bound by your Excel skills. **We do the lion's share of our analysis around the office with XLQ, which should tell you all you need to know.**

When you get into it, you realize that this program should cost a few hundred dollars a month. But it's actually less than $100 (yep, no monthly data charges or subscription fees... just a one-time charge for the program). The price is ridiculous. And you can download it for free and try it out before you buy (no credit card, or name or email address even needs to be given!). You have nothing to lose.

The only caveats are... You need to be pretty comfortable manipulating data and writing formulas in Excel. And you need to be willing to spend just a little time figuring out how XLQ works. Then, think of something you want to know (for example "I want to know the median Price-to-Sales ratio of the Nasdaq 100") and test it out. (For that example, you'll have to get the Nasdaq 100 names from www.nasdaq.com, and put them into Excel. Then use the XLQ formula.) If you really want to crunch numbers and test things on your own, we recommend giving XLQ a shot.

It goes against my rules. It goes against my objectives... and I don't have enough time per week to properly follow that one."

The more you put into this exercise, the more you'll get out of it. Give it a try. Your downside is 15 minutes with a pen in hand. Your upside is ending up like Mark Cook... who went from a farm boy to making millions in the markets, all because he was willing to try to learn from his mistakes.

Isn't your financial future worth 15 minutes with a piece of paper?

BEN FRANKLIN

Three Rules That Made Ben Franklin One of the Top 100 Richest Americans

Nothing but money is sweeter than honey. ~ Ben Franklin

Ben Franklin is famous for giving advice to aspiring entrepreneurs on ways to create and maintain a profitable business.

The Way to Wealth (published originally as part of his *Poor Richard's Almanac* in 1758) is an inspiring "how-to" pamphlet filled with Franklin's maxims and proverbs on how to build a successful enterprise.

What most people forget is that Franklin was also a successful investor after he retired from his printing business at the youthful age of 42. Despite war and numerous financial setbacks, he died a very wealthy man, and today is listed in the *Wealthy 100: The 100 Wealthiest Americans in History*.

Here's how he did it…

A Sound Investment Philosophy

In 1743, at the age of 42, Ben Franklin turned over his printing business to his partner David Hall, receiving an annual income for over 20 years afterwards. He never completely retired, however. He worked for the government as a postmaster, colonial agent in London and minister to France. Nevertheless, over the years, he built up a substantial fortune, and relied on his savings and investment income to pursue a gentleman's career in science, politics and community service.

Franklin built his investment retirement portfolio by saving, avoiding debt, placing well-collateralized loans (bonds) and investing in rental properties.

How did he manage his money?

Rule #1: Be an Optimistic Investor

Franklin ignored the doomsayers and profited from his prediction that America was destined to be a great, prosperous nation. An incurable optimist, Franklin was always bullish on America and life in general.

At the end of the War for Independence, he predicted, "America will, with God's blessing, become a great and happy country." The United States, he said, is "an immense territory, favored by nature with all advantages of climate, soil, great navigable rivers and lakes…. [and] destined to become a great country, populous and mighty."

He was critical of the doomsayers and complainers: "I saw in the public papers of different states frequent complaints of hard times, deadness of trade, scarcity of money, etc.," he wrote in 1785. "It is always in the power of a small number to make a great clamor. But let us take a cool view of the general state of our affairs, and perhaps the prospect will appear less gloomy than has been imagined."

In his *Autobiography*, he told the story of an elderly man who repeatedly predicted economic depression and a real estate collapse in Philadelphia, and warned Franklin to sell his printing house and his real estate holdings. Franklin ignored his advice and prospered. Eventually, he said, "I had the pleasure of seeing him give five times as much for one [piece of land]."

Know the signs of the times. Franklin recognized a great future for America, for he took advantage and invested in real estate, banking and other investments, even during a time of war. In order to make the right investment decisions, you need to have a sound view of the future. What is the future of America and global investing? Measure the pros and cons and make up your own mind. Personally, we've found there is usually some investment area worth pursuing, whether it be U.S. stocks, foreign investing, precious metals or real estate. There's always a bull market somewhere.

Rule #2: Beware of "Sure Deals"

Limit your speculative opportunities so as not to jeopardize your entire portfolio with speculations that promise "guaranteed" profits. You are bound to be misled and overly optimistic about the risk involved.

In 1769, Franklin joined with some partners/friends to seek a land grant of 20 million acres in the Ohio territory from the British Crown. His friends told him that the land grant was almost guaranteed. "We were daily amused with expectations that it would be completed at this or other time, but I saw no process made in it," he wrote a friend. His British agents frequently promised that the deal would take place "any day now," but five years later, nothing came of it. Ultimately, the partnership was never granted the land, and Franklin's investment went up in smoke.

Fortunately, Franklin's loss was small. He made the mistake of mixing money and friendship, but avoided the temptation to put too much money into a "sure deal."

Franklin's land grant investment is not unlike speculations some of you may be tempted to take in penny stocks and "private placement" with supposedly great prospects. Most never fulfill their grand promises. Diversify and minimize your exposure to these speculations. "Experience keeps a dear school, but fools will learn in no other."

Rule #3: How to Handle Financial Setbacks

<u>Diversify your holdings and limit your risks</u>. Franklin made it a point of having a wide variety of income sources, so that a loss in one would not destroy his entire portfolio. In addition to earning income from his role as minister and postmaster, he maintained seven or eight rental properties; earned interest-bearing bank accounts in Philadelphia, New York, London and Paris; invested in common stocks such as the Bank of North America, which paid a sizeable dividend; and occasionally loaned funds at interest to individuals and institutions.

His sizeable interest and rental income from bank accounts and real estate saved him from several severe financial setbacks during his years abroad.

In 1767, while a colonial agent to England, his long partnership in the printing business ended. "A great source of my income was cut off," Franklin wrote, forcing him and his wife to become more frugal in their spending habits. He limited himself to a "single dish" when dining at home.

In 1772, there was a banking crisis in England, but Franklin survived unscathed. "I only hazard a little using my credit with the bank... Being out of debt myself, my credit could not be shaken by any run upon me."

In 1774, Franklin suffered the most serious blow to his finances. As a result of the Hutchinson Letters scandal (where he sent confidential letters among British officials to America, where they were published), Franklin was vilified in England and fired from his job as postmaster and colonial agent, which amounted to a loss of £1,800 a year in income! Frugal living and their sizeable savings and income properties saved them from certain disaster. Late that year, his devoted wife Deborah died, and he was forced to return home.

Throughout, Franklin warned, "Revenue without economy is never enough." All of us are hit with financial setbacks from time to time. By always living within our means, even when those means occasionally shrink, we can always survive and prosper.

Despite a 10-year war and numerous financial setbacks, Franklin died a very rich man. At the end of his life, he said he wanted to be known as "a man who lived usefully," rather than "a man who died rich." It turns out that he became known for both!

DAVID RYAN
How To Make Three Moneymaking Secrets of a Champion Trader Work For You

David Ryan can teach you a few things about being a champion trader and winning in the stock market... With an astounding 161% return, Ryan won the stock division of the 1985 U.S. Investing Championship. To prove his results were no fluke, Ryan returned to the contest in 1986 and duplicated the feat, registering a 160% return.

We'll do a quick examination of Mr. Ryan's methods... and show you how we can still use three specific points of his 18-year-old strategy to produce triple-digit returns for ourselves.

Strategies of a Champion Trader Market Wizard

David got started early. He bought his first stock at 13. By 16, he was attending investment seminars and reading stock charts.

After graduating college, Ryan followed his dream. He went to famed investor William O'Neil and offered to do any job... just to get his foot in the door. He even offered to work for free!

All of David's hard work paid off... he eventually became a professional money manager and one of the elite traders interviewed by Jack Schwager in the famous best-seller, *Market Wizards*.

Ryan helped O'Neil make the "**buy high and sell higher**" strategy popular. This method of investing, which O'Neil calls the CANSLIM method, is one of the best stock-selection methods available to the individual investor, and Ryan is a master of it.

But there are a lot of good ways to pick stocks, and we're interested in aspects of Ryan's method that can apply to any investor or trader... whether they're using CANSLIM or not.

How Ryan Follows "The Golden Rule of Investing"

Despite being an expert stock picker and working seven days a week, Ryan claims he's right on only half of his picks. But he follows previously mentioned **David Ricardo's "Golden Rule of Investing,"** which, as we discussed earlier, is to "cut your losers short and let your winners ride." Ryan follows a rigid sell strategy of cutting his losses quickly... and making big money on a few stocks that double and triple in price.

Ryan's success is simple and can be followed by all of us. We learned three lessons from Ryan that we're constantly using to become more successful in the markets: Most traders are right "only" half the time. But they stay in the money by cutting losers quickly and riding the winners.

Ryan makes it a point to learn from every mistake he makes. Starting out, we tried to forget our losing trades. Now we keep a journal and go over every trade to learn how we could have done a little better.

Ryan knows what will cause him to sell a stock before he buys it. We follow his example and set a stop loss on every position. We think of it as "worst-case scenario" thinking. Of these, we think the best lesson we've learned from David Ryan is learning from our mistakes... It may not sound like a big "secret," but making sure you don't repeat investment mistakes will bring you much bigger returns than, say, the next best thing in biotechnology.

LEON LEVY
"The Caribou Factor" And How Human Emotions Can Drive Stock Prices

"Caribou, or their equivalents, always have a way of turning up" – Leon Levy, 50-year Wall Street veteran and author of *The Mind of Wall Street: A Legendary Financier on The Perils of Greed and the Mysteries of the Market*

Atlantic Richfield was already mentally cashing the huge checks it was about to receive as the owner of the Alaskan pipeline. Then, the company was hit by "The Caribou Factor"...

"Pardon me, but will the pipeline affect the migratory patterns of the caribou?" Someone asked this fateful question, which ended up financially humiliating Richfield. The company went from picturing profits to having to delay the project eight years and reschedule its debts. "The Caribou Factor" – or the idea that <u>you simply don't know what you don't know</u> when it comes to investing – is one of the many little gems from **Leon Levy's** fabulous book, *The Mind of Wall Street*.

The Market Does Ultimately Reflect Value

Levy is an outstanding communicator who has been a bigwig on Wall Street since the 1950s. While we can share more of Levy's lessons, it's much better to let Leon tell them himself.

First he asks, how we can even hope to make money in the markets... "If human nature makes markets inefficient and moody, and the Caribou Factor defeats the most exquisite analysis, it is natural to ask how anyone might hope to make money in the markets... "

He answers his own question: "A good idea, a long-term perspective, and the creativity to implement a strategy to profit from your insight are necessary to prosper in finance. But they are not sufficient.

None of these qualities will bear fruit unless you have the discipline to stay with your strategy when the market tests your confidence, as it inevitably will."

He goes on to say: "In such circumstances, it is easy to lose sight of the fact that ultimately, the market does reflect value, even if it may seem to lose its marbles for unbearably long periods. As the legendary value investor Benjamin Graham once put it, 'In the short term, the market is like a voting machine, reflecting a company's popularity, but over the long term, it more resembles a weighing machine, reflecting a company's true value.'

This is the aspect of the markets that allows the great investors to outdistance those who are lucky."

Human Emotions Are A Part of Investing... And We Need to Take Advantage

Levy's book touches on a deep, psychological dynamic of investing. Yet it is still easy to read. The recurring theme is that human emotions drive stock prices as much as the investment "fundamentals."

This idea makes many academics cringe. But we believe Leon Levy is right. We think his experience of 50-plus years in the trenches is as valuable as any academic study. And he says:

"Why should the market be any more perfect than the very human emotions and calculations that drive it? Investors overreact, and so do markets. Investors get swept up in moods, and so do markets. And this interplay creates investment

opportunities."

We need to recognize that human emotions are definitely a part of investing, and we need to take advantage of it. For example:

> "*Times of universal pessimism usually represent remarkable buying opportunities, and times of buoyant optimism are often a clarion call to sell. The simple reason... is that in times of universal optimism, most potential buyers of stock are already in the market, whereas in times of deep pessimism, investors are out of stocks, or trying to get out.*"

> "*It sounds simple... but it is not so easy to buy in a period of profound pessimism, even if your mind tells you (this) is the buying opportunity of the decade. For one thing all your friends are doing the opposite. For another, pessimism is based on plausible arguments.*"

He brings up another interesting idea that rings remarkably true in markets...

> "*Basically, we all live three lives: our life, the life of our parents, and that of our children. Events within our experience... remain the most visceral in memory. But events that lie beyond the horizon of these generations... don't have an immediate connection to our lives.*

> "*I might warn a (new kid on Wall Street) incessantly about the horrors of a crash or a bad market. But I will not likely make an impression on one who hasn't lived through that experience.*"

Amazingly, both novice investors and the most experienced investors will learn a great deal about how investing works by reading Levy's book.

In addition to pointing out the important role human emotions play in driving the stock market and other financial insight, *The Mind of Wall Street: A Legendary Financier on the Perils of Greed and the Mysteries of the Market* is a valuable guide into how to be a better investor, and entertaining as well. Anyone who seeks to acquire wisdom rather than information should check it out.

DR. HAROLD MARKOWITZ
How To Effectively Use Asset Allocation And Beat The Markets Year After Year

Asset Allocation is the process of developing the most effective – optimal – mix of investments. In this case, optimal means that there is not another combination of asset classes that is expected to generate a higher ratio of return to risk. And what does it consist of? Quite simply, it's breaking down your portfolio into different baskets, or classes of investments, to maximize returns and minimize risk. As the cliché goes, "Don't put all your eggs into one basket."

So let's take the first steps in breaking down your portfolio into baskets, or asset classes.

Where It All Started...

In 1990, **Dr. Harold Markowitz** won the Nobel Prize in Economics for his groundbreaking discovery of the math behind the **Gone Fishin' Portfolio**. Although many of the concepts used by Dr. Markowitz are hard to understand, he won the award because he showed how investors can master uncertainty and, at the same time, generate excellent investment results.

You don't even need a computer to implement this strategy. All the adjustments you'll need to make to your portfolio can be done once a year – with a single 15-minute phone call. The rest of the time, you're supposed to go fishing... or you can just spend your time however you choose. Because this strategy works.

Instead of struggling with trying to figure out when to get in and out of the market, do something simple: Spend 15 minutes a year on your asset allocation – a nominal amount of time when you consider the impact it can have on your portfolio... and your life.

How To Spread Your Eggs Around

Diversification is a strategy designed to reduce exposure to risk by combining a variety of investments which are unlikely to move in the same direction. In other words, you don't want to put all your money in investments that will perform similarly.

One of the best ways to diversify your portfolio is by placing your money into mutual funds. Because mutual funds are generally invested in a diverse portfolio of investments, they provide the greatest degree of diversification. By owning several investments, you lessen the chance that you'll suffer if one or two of them drops in value. One mutual fund can hold dozens or even hundreds of different securities at the same time.

The Oxford Club's Gone Fishin' Portfolio allows you to put this strategy to work through the lowest-cost group of mutual funds in the country, the Vanguard Group. Here's how you would asset allocate your "Nobel Prize" portfolio:

THE GONE FISHIN' PORTFOLIO
Vanguard Total Stock Market Index (VTSMX) – 15%
Vanguard Small-Cap Index (NAESX) – 15%
Vanguard European Stock Index (VEURX) – 10%
Vanguard Pacific Stock Index (VPACX) – 10%
Vanguard Emerging Markets Index (VEIEX) – 10%
Vanguard Short-term Bond Index (VFSTX) – 10%
Vanguard High-Yield Corporates Fund (VWEHX) – 10%
Vanguard Inflation-Protected Securities Fund (VIPSX) – 10%
Vanguard REIT Index (VGSIX) – 5%
Vanguard Precious Metals & Mining (VGPMX) – 5%

Notice that we have a 30% allocation to U.S. stocks. It is divided between small-cap and large-cap stocks. Likewise, the 30% allocation to international markets is evenly divided between Europe, the Pacific and Emerging Markets.

You might wonder how including some of these riskier assets – like emerging markets, gold and small-cap stocks, metals and mining – actually makes your portfolio less volatile. By combining these riskier – but non-correlated – assets, you actually increase your portfolio's return while reducing its volatility.

It is also important to note that The Gone Fishin' Portfolio is not exclusive to the Vanguard Group. We selected Vanguard as our family of funds simply because they have the lowest expense ratios (in fact, Vanguard occasionally restricts entry into certain of these funds). In an effort to maximize returns through Asset Allocation, reducing expenses with the Vanguard Group provides the best fund platform. But it can be used with any fund family.

If you'd like to imitate the above portfolio and don't know where to start, Schwab is a good company to contact: www.schwab.com. Simply use the same percentage breakout as noted above for your asset allocation. Then, from the list of funds available to you, select the ones that most closely mirror the Vanguard funds.

Who Should Consider The Gone Fishin' Portfolio?

For those of you who are conservative investors, who are retired or close to retirement, who need to exceed inflation while taking as little risk as possible – and who prefer casting purple worms to trading stocks – The Gone Fishin' Portfolio is designed with your serious money in mind.

Key Points To Remember

Asset allocation is time tested. It has worked and will

continue to work because it takes the guessing out of investing. Asset allocation is a Nobel Prize-winning strategy. No other strategy shares this seal of approval.

Research demonstrates that asset allocation accounts for approximately 90% of investment returns, making it nearly 10 times as important as stock picking and market timing combined. There is no other investment strategy that can boast the same.

The world's most successful and respected investors swear by it. As Paul Sturm of *Smart Money* puts it, asset allocation is "a simple strategy that comes as close to guaranteeing long-term success as anything I've seen."

Its benefits are unparalleled: significantly reduced expenses, protection against inflation, maximized returns with minimal risk, and the list goes on.

And the best part about it – it's simple. With The Gone Fishin' Portfolio, all you have to do is make one phone call – 15 minutes a year. It's worth considering...

JEREMY GRANTHAM
How To Survive the "Seven Lean Years"

"The idea behind the 'seven lean years' is that it is unrealistic to expect to overcome the several problems facing most developed countries, including the U.S., in fewer than several years..."
– REPORT TO HIS INVESTORS

Jeremy Grantham is CEO of the heavy-hitting, global investing management firm, GMO. And as writer of GMO's famous quarterly newsletter, he knows what he's talking about.

The above quote comes from a report Grantham wrote to his investors. He outlines current market period that we are entering into called the "seven lean years."

These lean years will require us to tighten our belts for an extended period of time as we (consumers, politicians and investors) recover from the financial crises, a drop in asset values, and an economic decline that drove the global market into the great recession.

He suggests that the road ahead will be rough, as the government slows spending and increases taxes, both factors that will slow the economic recovery. High unemployment, terrible local government finances and distressing news from Europe have driven the market down 13% from its high last year.

"The market might as well be called a fearful, speculative market. Low rates, although they tend to produce a feeding frenzy at the aggressive end of institutional investors, merely produce a feeling in ordinary individual investors somewhere between dejection and desperation."

But it's not all dark for Grantham, as he has uncovered some ways for us to capitalize on investor weariness.

Grantham, in his report, highlights the fact that normal equity investors (especially retirees) are so nervous that they have pulled out of the market, and in doing so, have moved their money into lower risk, fixed income schemes.

And this is exactly what Grantham wants us to see.

This move to fixed income scenarios has left certain high quality stocks at very cheap levels.

Grantham's advice: Know what is cheap and own it.

"High quality stocks are still cheap and have been for five years. These stocks might possibly spend much of the next several years under priced." Grantham recommends that investors overweigh their position, in high quality U.S. stocks while staying very light in other U.S. stocks.

And according to Grantham, for those who are still heavily exposed to U.S. stocks, emerging market equities are the next best play. Emerging equities still run circles around ours, and are listed as the second largest position to hold in Grantham's portfolio.

Grantham even goes on to express that forestry is an excellent position to have during turbulent times. Forestry equities are a good store value in case inflation runs away, and are historically superb defensive investments should the economy unravel.

So, if investment legend Jeremy Grantham is right about "seven lean years," this may be the toughest environment to invest in during his 40-year career. But there are still a few places to hide in stocks worldwide.

U.S. high quality stocks, emerging market equities and forestry could all see attractive lower prices as people continue to pull their money from the market and place them in lower fixed income schemes.

DENNIS GARTMAN:
The 10 Key Rules of Trading

Dennis Gartman doesn't work for a big financial firm or appear on the cover of magazines. (He doesn't even advertise.) He simply does what he's done for decades: He writes *The Gartman Letter*, the best daily newsletter on the markets:

Gartman's done many things right throughout the years... He bought bonds at the right time and then shorted them at the right time, too. He shorted oil at the top.

How does he do it? Fortunately Gartman shares that with us...

Once a year, on the day after Thanksgiving, Dennis publishes his **20 Rules of Trading**.

Here are some of Gartman's rules, in his own words...

1. Never, ever, ever add to a losing position. To do so will eventually and absolutely lead to ruin. Remember Long Term Capital Management and its legion of Nobel laureates who broke this rule repeatedly and went into forced liquidation. Learn this lesson... well and early!

2. Capital comes in two varieties: mental capital, and that which is in your account; of the two, mental capital is the more important. Holding losing positions costs measurable sums of actual capital, but it costs *immeasurable* sums of mental capital.

3. The objective is not to buy low and sell high, but to buy high and to sell higher. We can never know what price is "low." Nor can we know what price is "high." Always remember that Nortel fell from $85/share to $2 and seemed "cheap" all times along the way.

4. "Markets can remain illogical longer than you or I can remain solvent," is a brilliant statement from our good friend, Dr. A. Gary Shilling. Illogic often reigns and markets are inefficient despite what the academics try to tell us.

5. Sell that which shows the greatest weakness, and buy that which shows the greatest strength. Metaphorically, when bearish, throw rocks into the wettest paper sack, for they break most readily. In bull markets, ride the strongest winds.

6. Think like a fundamentalist; trade like a technician. It is imperative that we understand the fundamentals driving a trade, and also that we understand the market's technicals. When we do, then, and only then, should we trade.

7. Understanding psychology is usually more important than understanding economics. Markets are driven by human beings making human errors... and also making super-human insights.

8. Be patient with winning trades; be enormously impatient with losing trades. Remember, it is quite possible to make large sums trading/investing if we are "right" only 30% of the time, as long as our losses are small and our profits are large.

9. The hard trade is the right trade. If it is easy to sell, don't; and if it is easy to buy, don't. Do the trade that is hard to do and that which the crowd finds objectionable. Peter Steidelmeyer taught us this 30 years ago and it holds truer now than then.

10. There is never *one* cockroach. Bad news begets bad news, which begets even worse news.

It's not easy to know when to buy something of exceptional value when nobody else wants it, when an uptrend has begun.

You've got to think about both economics and human psychology... and you've to got to bear in mind both the fundamentals and the existing trend of a trade you're considering.

It's not easy. But this is the way to make money in the markets.

MICHAEL CHECKAN:
Invest in Gold Bullion and Historic Coins to Protect Your Savings

When it comes to gold and coins, there are few people with as much experience as Michael Checkan. Michael Checkan is President of Asset Strategies International, Inc. (ASI) and, for nearly three decades, has specialized in helping North Americans diversify assets internationally using the precious metals and foreign currency markets. Michael's an *Oxford Club* Pillar One Advisor and long-time friend.

Gold: The Ultimate Salvation Investment

There are a lot of reasons to buy gold.

Besides being lovely to behold, gold has an attractive combination of chemical and physical properties. It's virtually immune to the effects of air, water and oxygen. It will not tarnish, rust or corrode. And it is completely recyclable.

As *Time* magazine pointed out last week: *"It is an amazing metal. It can be pounded into a sheet so thin that light passes through it, yet the sheet won't crack. Gold can be stretched into wires thinner than a human hair, yet those wires will conduct electricity beautifully. Implant it in a human body in the form of a medical device, and it will resist the growth of bacteria. Gold is beautiful, pliable, ductile, and strong. The Stone Age, Bronze Age, and Iron Age all came and went, but gold is forever."*

In short, gold is used in everything from wedding bands, to fillings, to optic lasers – and more ...

- Thousands of mechanical devices require gold to ensure reliable performance over long periods.

- Billions of gold-coated electrical connectors are used throughout the computer, telecommunications and home appliance industries.

- Weather and communications satellites depend on gold-plated shields for protection from solar heat.

- Even the automobile industry depends on gold-coated contacts for sensors that activate air bag systems.

The price of "the barbarous relic" recently hit new all-time highs. But that has little to do with gold's fabulous properties.

Gold is also the color of anxiety. And investors are fearful right now ...

Why You Don't Want to See $5,000 Gold

Like all sensible investors, I own gold and gold shares. But I truly do not want to see the metal soar to $5,000 as some are predicting. Why?

Because, in all likelihood, that will be bad news indeed for the economy and our standard of living, not to mention the rest of your investment portfolio.

By and large, we are living in disinflationary times. Yes, the price of food and oil (and hence gas at the pump) have climbed over the past few years. But technology and deregulation have reduced the prices of many other things ...

- Look at the computing power you get for the money today. (And look how those computers lower costs for business.)

- Deregulation has brought down the price of airline tickets 25% – in constant dollars – over the past 15 years.

- When I went to college out of state many years ago, I

didn't call home that often for one simple reason: I couldn't afford it. But the break-up of Ma Bell has reduced the cost of long-distance calls to a pittance.

There is little threat of sharply higher inflation in the near term. But the longer term is a different story. And as the mess in Greece has proven, poor decision-making can cause long-term problems to suddenly show up on your doorstep.

Gold: Your No. 1 Economic Insurance Policy

Right now, gold is rising due to a lack of confidence in government and the reality that government bailouts don't necessarily fix problems. Sometimes, they just kick the can down the road a while.

All the European Union has done, for instance, is take the risk of owning Greek sovereign debt away from banks and other creditors and passed it on to taxpayers. Politicians often believe they can do magical things with other people's money.

- We all know what happens when an individual exercises long-term irresponsibility in his financial affairs: personal bankruptcy.

- We've all seen what happens when a highly leveraged business can no longer service its debt: corporate bankruptcy.

- And in the years just ahead, Westerners may very well see what massive fiscal irresponsibility does to national governments, their debt ratings and their currencies.

No one can say exactly how and when this will play out. But there is a distinct possibility that gold will be your salvation investment.

That means – just like property and casualty insurance – that gold is something you really can't afford not to own.

CHUCK BUTLER:
How to Profit from Foreign Bonds While Keeping Your Account in the U.S.

Chuck Butler is part of the team that launched EverBank(www.everbank.com), one of the nation's largest online banks. As the Senior Vice President of EverBank World Markets. He oversees the trading desk and operations for over 12,000 individual and corporate clients, both in the United States and abroad, who look to EverBank for FDIC-insured *World Currency Deposit Accounts*, and *Single Currency and Index CDs*.

Please excuse us for always assuming that most people know how to buy foreign currency bonds. It is a common trap to fall into. If you have been doing something for 20 years, you start assuming that it is commonplace. We realize, of course, that it is not.

Very few Americans have anything outside of the U.S. dollar, and this is unfortunate. You think nothing of buying insurance for your life or your house, but almost no one insures themselves against a fall in the very currency that they work so hard to get and save and invest in.

But anyone who is familiar with the dollar's long-term slide against the other major currencies – as well as many emerging market currencies – knows they are losing valuable purchasing power.

Two Ways To Buy Foreign Bonds in the U.S.

Although it's previously been difficult for most Americans to diversify outside of the U.S. dollar, fortunately Everbank has made this task much easier while still providing FDIC insurance. Everbank offers:

- **Single-currency CDs:** Open a CD in one of 17 offered foreign currencies and earn interest at local rates for the particular currency.

- **Multi-currency CDs:** Open a single CD comprised of multiple currencies—each strategically designed to focus on a specific regional strength, and/or geopolitical and economic development.

- **World Currency Access Account:** The choice if you're looking to diversify your financial portfolio globally against a depreciating U.S. dollar without locking yourself into a fixed term.

If you'd rather try and keep your account entirely with your existing broker you could:

Call your own broker and see if he does large enough global bond business that the minimums could be put below 10,000 units for you. It probably is too much to hope that you could get in for just 1,000 units, but stranger things have happened.

We know that Schwab does a brisk business in foreign bonds now. Maybe your broker does as well. Another thought: Ask your broker if he can buy one-year T-bills in foreign currencies. It is possible that the minimums could be lower. We wouldn't be too hopeful, however.

So start thinking globally—diversify your portfolio with the world's major currencies. Benefit from the appreciation of currencies against the U.S. dollar and earn interest rates from around the world.

DANIEL DREW:
Three 150-Year-Old Investing Rules That Will Help You Grow Rich Today

Daniel Drew was bigger than **Warren Buffett** and **Alan Greenspan** *combined* back in his day...

Sure, he was a real dirt-bag... He cheated his fellow church parishioners out of money. He was a director of one of the biggest companies in America, yet consistently bet against it in the stock market for huge profits. In short, he was a bad dude.

But Drew became one of the richest men in America through trading stocks in the mid to late 1800s. In many ways, times were much different... Drew rode a horse to Wall Street! And there was no SEC and no Federal Reserve. But in many ways, things were exactly the same then as they are today...

And the secrets Drew used nearly 150 years ago to build his fortune are the exact same ones that work right now. Drew revealed those secrets in *The Book of Daniel Drew*. Let's consider a few of them today, and how we can use them to generate wealth like he did...

Drew's Three Secrets: Clean Strategies from a Dirty Player

1. "The money market is the key to the stock market. They who control the money rate also control the stock(s)." He's right... but it's amazing that he understood this 150 years ago... before there was a Federal Reserve controlling the money rate. For proof of how right he is even today, consider this...

When interest rates are rising, you don't make money in stocks. Over the 17 years from 1964 to 1981, the Dow (the stock market) gained less than one point (874.1 to 875). During that time, interest rates rose from 4% to 14%. Now consider the next 17 years – from 1981 to 1998. Interest rates did nothing but fall. And the Dow went from 875 to over 9,000.

In January of 2005, then-Federal Reserve Chairman Alan Greenspan forced interest rates to extremely low levels. So stock prices rallied.

Daniel Drew knew the secret 150 years ago… he who controls the money market controls the stock market.

2. *"The way to make money in Wall Street is to calculate on what the common people are going to do, and then go and do just the opposite."*

Drew was a master of this. If he were around in 2007, he would have been betting on a crash, as "the common people" were all buying stocks.

When you can determine that most people are all doing the same thing with their money, don't consider it as a comfortable investment – chances are, the big gains are already behind you there.

3. *"I ought to have (closed my position) without a moment's delay – cut short your losses and let your profits run, is the rule."*

Wow… we're confident the "cut your losses and let your profits run" rule is the difference between successful investors and those who'll never make any money. It amazes us that this "golden rule" was known and solidly established 150 years ago by men like David Ricardo and Daniel Drew, yet still applies today

You'd think that a rule so well known wouldn't work anymore. But people never seem to learn… most folks take a quick profit when they see it, and they hang onto their losses –

exactly the opposite of what they should be doing.

So let's review…

- "The money market is the key to the stock market. They who control the money rate also control the stock(s)."
- "The way to make money in Wall Street is to calculate on what the common people are going to do, and then go and do just the opposite."
- "Cut short your losses and let your profits run, is the rule."

These rules made Daniel Drew enormously wealthy. They were the path to real wealth in investing 150 years ago. **And they are still the best rules to follow today.**

They say human nature doesn't change – the emotions of greed and fear still overpower the rational ideas of the "right" way to do things, like invest.

When you get caught up in the excitement of an investment or of the times, go back and review these three rules. If you consistently stick to them, you might just join Daniel Drew in the ranks of legendary investors.

ALEXANDER GREEN
Five Ways To Lower Your Risk and Improve Your Returns

For months, equity investors have been complaining about what a volatile – and often frustrating – year this has been for stocks.

High unemployment, ongoing housing foreclosures and an economy in the dumps have taken their toll on stocks.

With this in mind, now is a good time to review our strategies for reducing your portfolio risk.

These five reminders can do more than anything to keep your money safe and your investments sound…

#1. Buy quality. In market downturns, dividend-paying blue chips hold up better than up-and-comers. Large caps will do better than small caps. And value generally does better than growth.

If anything in your equity portfolio needs to go, look at your small-cap stocks, unprofitable companies and other more speculative issues.

#2. Diversify broadly. Some members comment occasionally about the large number of recommendations in our Oxford Trading Portfolio. But it has two advantages: It increases your chances of holding a big winner, and it leads to less volatility than holding just a handful of stocks.

#3. Asset allocate. We've beaten this drum so many times, we're half expecting an invitation from the Choctaw Nation in Oklahoma. But it simply can't be said often enough. Your asset allocation is your single most important investment decision.

We currently recommend that 60% of your money is in stocks; 10% should be in high-grade bonds; 5% should be in real estate investment trusts; 10% should be in inflation-adjusted Treasuries; 5% should be in gold shares; and 10% should be in high-yield bonds.

#4. Follow our position sizing strategy. Never invest more than 4% of your equity portfolio in a single stock – at least initially. There's nothing worse than having a serious dent in your net worth simply because one stock fell out of bed.

#5. Use our trailing stop discipline. Whenever a stock in our Oxford Trading Portfolio falls back 25% from its high – or from our entry price – we put out a Safety Switch Alert, telling you to sell at market to protect your profits or your principal.

This is simply a tool to cut your losses and let your profits run. I've never seen great results come any other way. Looking over this list, you'll notice there are no Fibonacci numbers. No urgent market signals. No prophesies of doom or euphoria. And that's exactly the point.

The principles of successful money management have stood the test of time. They're battle-tested. That's why they're principles... not fads.

JEFF WINN:
A Stock Market Investment That Doesn't Lose Value

"You really mean I can't lose money?"

Jeff Winn, Wealth Protection Director for International Assets Advisory, has been getting this question a lot lately.

With all the volatility in the market these days and in light of some of the big losses investors have suffered recently, it's no surprise that an investment that won't lose value is very attractive. And Jeff understands why clients are skeptical of this claim... but his answer always remains the same.

"That's right. At the end of a year, your principal will never go down," he replied.

We know there's no free lunch in this world. But we also know that the way to make money is to limit your downside risk (i.e. prevent a "catastrophic" loss), and leave your upside potential as unlimited as possible.

With the investment Jeff is **talking** about – called **equity-indexed annuity** – this is all possible. So we sat down with Jeff to find out more.

Jeff Winn: Look at it this way... If you invest $100,000 in the first year, and the market falls by 20%, the value of your investment will be $100,000. And in the second year, if the market goes up by 20%, then your investment will be worth $120,000.

Oxford Club: **I find that a ridiculously good offer... your portfolio never has to recover from a fall. No downside and all the upside: That doesn't seem right...**

How can it be possible?

JW: Well, you get *almost* all of the upside of the stock market… In the investment I'm talking about, you're capped to a 2.7% gain in the stock market in any one-month. Let me give an extreme example… If the market is flat for 11 months, and then goes up 12% in December, then you're only credited for 2.7% for the year. As another extreme example, if the market is up 2% every month for the whole year, than you never bumped into the cap and get to keep all those gains.

OC: So this thing is called an equity-indexed annuity, huh? I don't know a lot about annuities. But I used to hear that fees were high. What's the story with annuities?

JW: There is generally a "surrender charge," which usually declines every year and eventually disappears in seven years' time, in the equity-indexed annuity I've been recommending. If you can hold for seven years, then you will have gotten most of the upside and none of the downside of the stock market, with the only 'cost' being the fact that your upside was limited to 2.7% in any month. That's a fair trade-off to me. For the full story, you might want to check out Jack Marrion's website… I did. Jack Marrion is the industry watchdog. He runs a site called www.indexedannuities.com. Here are a few recent points from Jack:

- No index annuity owner has ever lost a dime due to market downturn.

- No index annuity owner has ever lost a dime because a carrier failed.

- Unlike bonds, index annuities don't lose value when interest rates rise.

- An index annuity lets you take advantage of market drops.

So what's the real risk? Jack Marrion says: *"The biggest risk an index annuity owner faces is that they might have earned a higher return in another vehicle (but then again, hindsight's always 20/20)."*

The idea with index annuities is that, over time, they'd beat your fixed investments like CDs and bonds, but may underperform the stock market. It's quite possible that these index annuities could beat both fixed investments and the stock market over the next few years. And they would do so with less risk – as neither stocks nor bonds guarantee that you'll make money.

Three Steps To Get You Started With Index Annuities

These things are not right for everyone. But if you're over 50 and not particularly optimistic about the stock market… or if you like the idea of guaranteed minimum returns with a stock-like upside, we recommend you do three things:

- Spend a good amount of time on Jack Marrion's website: www.indexannuity.org, where he explains the ins and outs of index annuities. Once you've done that, determine which indexed annuity might be appropriate for you, then…

- Contact our recommended financial planner Jeff Winn of International Assets in Orlando, FL, at 800.432.4402, or e-mail jwinn@iaac.com. Jeff will take good care of you. He can answer your questions and meet your financial planning needs.

Lastly, be aware that we don't consider ourselves experts in this area, and we don't own nor have ever bought an equity-indexed annuity. Please make sure you do plenty of your own homework to determine if this is right for you…

CHRIS ANDERSON:
Three Factors For Determining Exactly How Much To Invest

Chris Anderson, founder of 99% Trading Corporation, firmly believes that computer testing and analysis can significantly improve the performance of many investors and traders. But no amount of investigating and examining will pay off if you don't know exactly how much to invest. So, we want to share a few of Chris' ideas that will help improve your investment results...

Two Questions Chris Asks Before Using a Trading System

First, Chris wants to see the historical results of any investment system in black and white before he considers following that investment advice. Chris likes to get as long a track record as possible. Then he tests how it did...

Do you do this? We think most investors don't.

After he runs the investment system through some tests and discovers that it works, the big questions are: 1) Do I trade this approach since it made money in the past... and 2) How does it fit into my current investments?

Chris says that once you know a system makes money, it still doesn't mean you should trade it, as it may be much too volatile for your risk tolerance.

Once Chris knows an investment approach works, then he further refines how to use it... He tests exactly how much to put in each trade to get maximum return with minimum risk. This could actually be different for different investors.

Chris says it comes down to three things:

- Your investment goals
- Your risk tolerance
- The historical performance of your system

Chris is thinking about a part of the trade that very few are thinking of... He is answering the question, "Exactly how much should I put in a trade based on this investment system?" Figuring out exactly how much to invest in each position in a system is difficult. But Chris finds the challenge fun. And this is a question you should ask yourself before using any trading system.

MICHAEL STEINHARDT:

How To Turn $10,000 Into $5 Million By Going Against the Professionals

$10,000 invested with **Michael Steinhardt** in 1967 would have been worth nearly $5 million dollars when he called it quits in 1995.

He traded with conviction. As an example, he went short (to profit from the downside) in the best companies in America, right before the 1973-1974 crash. While many of the "star" fund managers of the day lost 80% or 90% over that time, Steinhardt increased his investors' money by nearly 60%. Then, at the end of 1974, Steinhardt "picked the bottom nearly perfectly" in his own words.

How did he do it? The key is in this quote from his book, *No Bull: My Life In and Out of Markets: "When the world wants to buy only (bonds), you can almost close your eyes and (buy) stocks."*

First, let's consider how Steinhardt made such a fortune for investors, including what might work now. Then, we'll share Steinhardt's four pieces of required homework in order to have a successful stock pick.

Steinhardt's Four Million-Dollar Rules To Making an Investment

If an analyst was going to present an idea to Steinhardt, that analyst knew the rules... He needed to be able to tell him, in two minutes, four things:

- The idea
- The consensus view
- The "variant perception"
- A trigger event

Steinhardt's definition of variant perception is, "*a well-founded view that is meaningfully different from the market consensus.*"

Steinhardt said, "*In those instances where there was no variant perception… I generally had no interest and would discourage investing.*"

See if you have all four rules covered for each. Be honest with yourself… do you own Microsoft or Pfizer because your friends think they're good? Or do you truly have a "variant perception?"

Think of new stocks you buy in Steinhardt's terms and maybe you'll find a few Steinhardt-type profits…

PETER DRUCKER
Why Peter Drucker Likes Frugal Entrepreneurs

In the early 1990s, *Oxford Club* Advisory Panelist **Mark Skousen** met and interviewed Peter Drucker for *Forbes*. He talked about Japan, and warned that the Japanese were headed for trouble and a long slump because they had become too bureaucratic and arrogant. He was right, as he was on many of his predictions.

Investors who followed his wise advice avoided Japan as an investment – and saved a lot of money.

Below, you'll find three more bits of Drucker's wisdom you can use today...

1. Invest In Entrepreneurial Companies

Invest in companies that are entrepreneurial, and avoid companies that are too bureaucratic.

Drucker, an Austrian economist, was a big believer in entrepreneurship, innovation and capital formation. He favored companies that took big risks and spent lots of capital on R&D. He hated companies that had nothing better to do than repurchase their stock, or pay out big dividends.

He was born in Austria in 1909, and his roots stayed with him all his life. His favorite economist was fellow Austrian Joseph Schumpeter, a believer in entrepreneurship and a dynamic model of capitalism ("creative destruction").

2. Curb Spending... And Invest More!

You can never save and invest too much. Drucker disliked big spenders, heavy borrowers and governments that couldn't balance budgets. The smart investor always lives within his means, and uses his savings productively – either in expanding his business, or investing in other people's successful businesses (i.e., buying quality stocks).

He blamed Keynesian economics for an unhealthy anti-saving mythology, causing "under-saving on a massive scale" in the West, both by individuals and government.

Government, he said, is only good at three things: Inflation, taxation and making war! He once bluntly told a U.S. president, "government is obese, muscle-bound and senile." Yet he wasn't against government, per se. He wanted a strong, healthy, vigorous government. To accomplish this goal, he recommended privatization of many state services.

In fact, he and Robert Poole (founder of *Reason* magazine) invented the term "privatization." He was a longtime supporter of privatizing pension plans, both by government and corporations (he preferred defined-*contribution* plans like 401(k)s and IRAs, rather than defined-*benefit* plans such as Social Security and corporate pensions).

3. Locate Bull Markets Around the World

Be an optimist. Drucker was encouraged by the collapse of the Soviet Marxist model in the early 1990s, which helped developing countries privatize, denationalize and open up their domestic economies to foreign capital. He recommended investing in emerging market economies. Not surprisingly, stock markets at that time boomed in Russia, Eastern Europe, Asia and Latin America.

In the U.S., he was a big supporter of tax cuts, especially tax breaks for capital investment and entrepreneurship. The corporate income tax, said Drucker, is the "most asinine of taxes" and should be abolished.

Business as the Ideal "Social Institution"

Finally, he felt that the private sector – major corporations and nonprofit institutions – was the only "free, non-revolutionary way" to a stable, prosperous society. Business and private charities provided a superior alternative to socialism and big government. According to Drucker, only business could assume the social responsibilities such as job security, training and educational opportunities, and social benefits such as health care, retirement, paid vacation, etc.

When he first suggested the private sector as the ideal "social institution" after World War II, he was considered a renegade. (Even General Motors thought he was nuts.) But once again, he was proven right.

BENJAMIN GRAHAM:
Using "Graham's Number" To Buy Cash at a Discount

Benjamin Graham is commonly known as the father of value investing. In the 1930s, he wrote the bible on securities analysis, which is still the main book on the subject today. Graham was legendary investor **Warren Buffett's** mentor, having taught him in college at Columbia.

Trading coach **Van Tharp** says that during the worst bear market of the 1930s, Ben Graham averaged returns of 17% a year. And during the great bear market the dozen years before the bottom in 1982, the average annual return on stocks meeting Graham's criteria was 33.7% a year, according to one study.

So how did he do it? "Graham's Number," one of the most popular investment concepts, is easily boiled down: Buy cash at a discount (actually, cash and things that can be easily turned into cash – in other words, Net Current Assets). Graham's idea is that if you can pay as little as two-thirds of "cash" for a stock, you've really got nothing to lose.

How It Works

Here's how you get to "Graham's Number" for any company: It's simply Current Assets minus Total Debts.

Current assets are defined as anything that can be turned into cash within a year. Total debt is self-explanatory. So another way to describe "Graham's Number" is: It is simply a company's Net Current Assets. Yet another way to think of it is basically what cash is left if you were to pay off all debts. And, if you find a company that's going for two-thirds – or 66% of – the value of its cash, that's a value.

As you might expect, it's difficult to find stocks this cheap. To give you an idea of how stringent the criteria are: Out of the thousands of stocks out there, only a tiny handful qualify as good value investments under Graham's criteria.

Determining "Graham's Number" on Your Own

First we need to get the Current Assets and the Total Liabilities of **Company XYZ**. You can do this in Yahoo! Finance (www.yahoo.com, click on "Finance"). Then enter the stock symbol of the company your looking for and then click on Financials.

Let's say for Company XYZ, here's what we find on the Balance Sheet: $3.6 billion Current Assets and $2.1 billion Total Debts. Therefore "Graham's Number" (or net current assets) is $1.5 billion. Now we need to consider the market value of Company XYZ (also called the "market cap" and calculated as number of shares times current market price)... Is XYZ an extraordinary bargain, selling at less two-thirds of its net current assets?

Let's say Company XYZ's market value is $1.3 billion at the moment. So you can buy the stock for less than its net current assets – you're buying at a discount to cash, in a sense. A bargain.

However, in order to buy at two-thirds of Graham's number (1.5 billion, in this case), you'd want XYZ's market value to be at $1.0 billion or less (66% of 1.5 billion). Cutting to the chase, the current price for XYZ ($6.50, which equates out to $1.3 billion in market cap) isn't at the 66% level we'd need to make this a "Graham's Number" investment. The price will have to come down to $5.00 per share for that.

You can do this homework yourself to find stocks that meet this criteria. It will likely take a little wrestling of stock screeners and spreadsheets, or checking out the Value Line. Paying two-thirds of net current assets is the idea behind "Graham's Number." Buying stocks this cheap sure sounds like a no-brainer. Consider how your favorite stocks stack up…

LOUIS BASENESE
How To Make More Money By Choosing Dividend Stocks: Six Steps For Finding Safe, High-Yield Investments

You don't want to hear it, but the smartest play right now is in dividend stocks... Most folks believe the saying: "The more you risk, the more you can make... "

Not so fast... There are ways to beat the markets by actually risking less... For example, Louis Basenese, Chief Investment Strategist for *The White Cap Report* and former Wall Street consultant, knows that buying high-yield dividend stocks actually beats buying risky "growth" stocks over the long run. Amazing!

The common wisdom is that you have to invest in risky things like tech stocks and other growth companies to really generate big returns. Louis knows it's the opposite... buying "boring businesses" with high-yielding dividends at cheap values is where you make your money over the long run. It sounds counterintuitive, but we think Louis has a point. Here's why...

The latest tally from famed professor, Jeremy Siegel – author of the investing classic, *Stocks for the Long Run* – proves that dividend stocks are still the best investment. Period.

Yet everyone still loves to dog them for being boring and slow growers.

Big mistake.

How a 3.7% Gain Means An Extra $370,000

In his study, Professor Siegel sorted the S&P 500 stocks by

dividend yield, dating back to 1957, and recorded the return of the top 100 dividend-yielders versus the bottom 100 for each year.

The result?

Investing in the top yielders delivered an annualized average return of 12.5%, compared to an average return of 8.8% for the lowest yielders.

Now, a 3.7% difference might not seem like much. But if you started with a $1,000 portfolio and reinvested all the dividends, it would be worth $450,000 today. That compares to only $80,000 without the extra 3.7% pop.

But how do we go about finding safe, dividend-paying stocks in this market?

After all, companies keep slashing dividends by a record amount. From 2007 to 2009, total dividend payments slumped by $72 billion – the worst decline in over 50 years.

Lou's Six Steps to Finding the Best Dividend-Yielding Stocks

When looking for the best high-yield dividend stocks, the simple answer might sound a bit backwards: Don't chase yield.

This is because a high yield typically indicates that there's a higher risk of the dividend being cut or – even worse – being eliminated altogether.

Instead, focus on companies with the following six characteristics:

- **Simple Business:** The fewer moving parts, the fewer things that can go wrong, thus sapping cash intended for dividend payments. So focus on companies with businesses that you understand, rather than massive corporations that have dozens of (often puzzling) operating segments.

- **Steady Demand:** After identifying companies with simple business models, the next step is to verify that there is demand for the product(s). After all, a company needs a steady stream of cash so it can afford to pay dividends to shareholders. Stick to industries or sectors with recession-proof or recession-resistant demand (food, alcohol, tobacco, healthcare, etc.)

- **Cash Flow Positive:** If a company isn't generating cash each quarter, the only way to pay a dividend is by borrowing or tapping into cash reserves. Such practices aren't sustainable over the long-term – and the dividend will eventually be cut.

- **High Cash Balance:** Speaking of cash… it's still king. Especially when it comes to maintaining a dividend. Consider it insurance against any unexpected slowdowns. At a minimum, insist on enough cash to cover one quarter's worth of dividends.

- **Minimal Need for Credit:** Securing credit in this market is extremely difficult. Accordingly, I recommend focusing on companies that don't need to raise significant amounts of capital. That's because when interest rates rise, so will their interest payments. I also suggest you look at companies with a reasonable or low debt load. This ensures that interest payments won't sap money intended for us.

- **Earnings Buffer:** Insist on a dividend payout ratio (annual dividends divided by annual net income) of 80% or less. This will provide ample wiggle room for the company to pay the dividend in the event of an unexpected slowdown. Or even better, to justify raising the dividend.

Now that you know how to find the most profitable dividend stocks... add a few to your portfolio. A diversified dividend-paying portfolio offers you additional safety, while still providing attractive yields and monthly dividend checks.

KATHLEEN PEDDICORD
Maximizing Real Estate Returns by Going Global

Kathleen Peddicord has quite possibly seen more internation-al real estate opportunities in out-of-the-way places than anyone on the planet. An Ireland-based U.S citizen and former publisher of International Living, *Kathleen is the woman to turn to when it comes to overseas property investing. Following Kathleen's advice on investing in international real estate can pay off immensely. Here's what she had to say...*

Five Advantages of International Real Estate – And Three Ways You Can Profit

Most U.S. investors are overlooking what I've found to be a simple truth: <u>The best deals and the biggest opportunities in real estate today are not to be found within U.S. borders.</u>

Take U.S. coastlines… Sure, America has some gorgeous beaches… and stunning seaside properties. But there's a severely limited supply, especially of Grade-A beachfront real estate… and a burgeoning demand, especially among baby boomers. Even if your budget isn't small, you'll have trouble finding a seaside getaway on either U.S. coast that could be called a bargain.

Almost all resort property in the U.S. is already priced beyond the means of the average buyer. But the U.S. doesn't have a monopoly on nice beaches. Indeed, some of the most desirable property in the world right now does not happen to sit within the confines of U.S. borders.

I've been looking at the world this way for a long time… seeking out top-shelf real estate in undervalued markets, places where some special combination of factors – economic, political, etc. – allows you to buy at a discount (rather than a premium, as you're forced to do in the U.S. right now). International real estate offers five advantages over domestic real estate:

1. Global real estate investments can appreciate faster than U.S. real estate. Because you're buying at a discount, there is higher ceiling for appreciation. Furthermore, with today's technology, many people can work from anywhere on the planet. Why work in a Peoria, IL suburb when you could work and live just as easily on the beach in Belize? More and more people are thinking this way... and the market for non-U.S. real estate will continue to appreciate accordingly.

2. Global real estate offers you a safe alternative if things go bad (or worse) in the U.S. Many Americans fear for their constitutional rights, which seem to be taking a back seat to Homeland Security. I'd argue that no government is "good" government... but many around the world are much less intrusive than that in the U.S.

3. Global real estate is an easy way to move some of your assets offshore. Few restrictions are placed on Americans related to the purchase of property overseas. And once you own property abroad, it's extremely difficult for the government, creditors or anyone else to get at it.

4. Your real estate investment can double as a personal retreat, part-time residence or vacation getaway. You can take enjoyment from it while it's appreciating in value... generating rental returns... safeguarding your net worth.

5. Global real estate investing can open the doors and broaden your horizon to a new lifestyle. How many investments work like that? Not many that I can think of. Plus, the wealth you build with your real estate investments abroad will go much further in a fast growing developing economy than in the States.

There's a global migration to places with great weather, little pollution, good views, a relaxed lifestyle and low prices. Indeed, the baby boom generation is more open to the idea of a new life abroad than any generation before it... and baby boomers have not only the inclination, but also the money and the time to pursue dreams of life in some far-off paradise.

It's possible today to live, work, relax or retire anywhere you want. The investors who recognize this trend and identify its path will profit most.

Finding What's Right For You

As an international real estate investor, you can primarily make money in three ways:

1. By purchasing property (land, a house, an apartment building, etc.), adding value and flipping.

2. By investing in properties (a house, an apartment, a resort unit) that produce rental income (which exceeds holding costs) that can help compound capital appreciation.

3. By investing in raw land that you have reason to believe will appreciate in value in the coming years. This is a longer-term, buy-and-hold strategy.

DAN DENNING
The Best Foreign Stock Pick For the Next 10 Years

Alexander Green counts "Bull Hunter" Dan Denning among the sharpest guys he knows. Alex sat down with Dan to get a glimpse of the Bull Hunter at work. During the course of the interview, Dan shared what he believes is the best stock for the next 10 years...

Alexander Green: Dan, what would you tell someone just getting into investing right now?

Dan Denning: The first thing they'd have to realize is that there's very little money in the market right now. But people still have to do something with their money. So what I've been doing for the last year is making different market calls... If there's not a lot of money sloshing around in the market, which there isn't right now, you have to find where the value is.

For example, on the income side, money has been flowing into Australia, where short-term interest rates are in excess of 5%. Another place is raw materials, and I like those. In terms of regions, I like the Far East, in particular Australia, because of the long-term dynamics in the China story and the growth of Asia.

My approach starts with "where are the values now?" at the macro level... "Are we in a bull market or a bear market?" And then my investment selection is dictated by that call. So then I figure out what asset to be in, what region to be in, etc.

AG: So, specifically, how are you playing the Australia and raw materials ideas?

DD: Normally I like to buy exchange-traded funds, but

there wasn't a good way to buy raw materials through an ETF. I am going long the Australian stock market ETF (Amex: EWA), because Australia is a commodity-producing country. Australia is a great story, as a commodity-producing country with attractive interest rates, so it's attracting foreign capital.

And it's sort of a peripheral China play. For example, **BHP Billiton** (NYSE: BHP) has been on a tear recently because Australia has been exporting a tremendous amount of raw materials to China.

AG: Dan, shifting gears, what's your answer when you get asked about the "traditional" investment advice of having 70% in stocks and 30% in bonds?

DD: I generally don't talk about allocations in the conventional sense. Given that I think we're in a serious bear market where stocks could fall dramatically, I don't recommend owning a lot of stocks.

If you pressed me, I'd recommend 25% in gold stocks. I'd recommend 15% in bonds, through exchange-traded funds. They're a great way to get invested in fixed income without having to buy bonds themselves, and they're easy for individual investors to understand and buy.

We recommend a handful of exchange-traded funds, which are Asian country funds. Japan, Taiwan, Singapore, and then the Templeton Emerging Markets Fund (NYSE: EMF), which I think you own as well, Alex. [*Editor's note: Dan's right – we do own EMF in our Oxford All-Star Portfolio.*] It'd be 25% in stock-like investments. That's about as much as I feel comfortable with in stocks. I also recommend a good-sized position in stock market puts (a kind of option), expecting a fall in stock prices.

AG: How do you get out of a position?

DD: I do use trailing stops to get out of a position, but not all the time. I actually don't recommend them with the gold stocks. Even in a bad bear market for the general market, the commodity stocks will weather the storm better and still be worth owning at the end of the day. That's my thinking now, at least.

The thing is I don't follow gold necessarily as a commodity; I follow it as money... as the anti-dollar. So that's the basis of our gold stocks.

BILL GROSS:

The King of Bonds is Taking Up Stocks as A Better Long-Term Investment

"If your talking about the next 10, 15, 20 years, there's certainly the recognition that assets will grow faster in stocks. Over the long term, stocks return more than bonds when appropriately priced at the beginning of an investment period." – "BOND KING" **BILL GROSS**

Bill Gross is a bond genius… And he'd better be, as he runs the world's biggest fixed-income fund. As CEO of Pacific Investment Management Co. (Pimco), Bill Gross's Total Return Fund beat 97% of its rivals in the past decade.

So it's no wonder that *Morningstar Inc. named him the fixed-income fund manager of the decade, after earning a 10-year annualized return of 7.7% in Pimco's Total Return Fund.* And *SmartMoney* magazine named Gross one of the "SmartMoney 30" most influential people in investing.

So why is the "Bond King" moving out of bonds?

According to Pimco the three-decade rally in bonds— the securities that made Gross famous – are fizzling out. The rally is coming to an end as nations sell record amounts of debt to finance their deficits, spurring a come back to inflation and rising interest rates.

"Bonds have seen their best days," states Gross, who anticipates 4% to 5% gains as the new normal.

As Bill and his colleagues see it, mounting deficits and tighter financial regulations will dampen growth in the euro zone and the U.S. for the next three to five years. Meanwhile, emerging-markets like China and Brazil will continue to thrive with their growing middle classes and stable levels of government debt.

Pimco's take, along with many other experts, is that the U.S. will see growth of 2% or less in the next several years, hampered by regulation and debt.

The yield on the 10-year Treasury note was 2.5% in late August, a one year low. The future of low returns in bonds is making PIMCO, which is traditionally a bond-shop, switch its fundamental fund management approach into equities.

With $1.1 trillion in assets, Pimco has plans to integrate ten new equity funds in the near future that focus on global strategies. These new funds will purchase undervalued securities in emerging markets and Europe.

39 years after he started Pimco, Gross highlights that these new funds are showing a sign of his own evolution along with the new market. Gross stated, "I'm 66 now and recognize there are lots of different pieces to a puzzle, and they each have a right to a place in the capital markets."

Investors should recognize this evolution as well and look at carefully allocating their assets into stocks.

CHRIS WEBER
The "Max Yield" Strategy… How to Make a $425,000 Profit on the World's Currencies

Put your hand in your pocketbook or wallet. What do you find? Dollars, of course.

What's in your savings account, your money-market fund? What is your mortgage valued in? How do you express the value of your stocks and bonds?

Unless you're one of those rare Americans who has opened a foreign bank account or bought a modest amount of foreign currencies or securities – everything you own is in dollars. And right now, that could be incredibly detrimental to your financial well-being. Why? Because for the last few years, the U.S. dollar has been losing steam. In fact, since 2003, the dollar has lost 19% of its value against the euro, and 26% against the New Zealand dollar.

Think about that. If everything you own is in dollars, and the dollar has lost 15% of its value, even if you did nothing at all with your money, your net worth is just 85% of what it was in June of 2003, relative to what it could have been had you diversified.

Cash Out on the Dollar… And Cash In On the World

So what's the solution? Get out of the dollar, obviously. But where? How? Well, that's what you're about to learn here with the "Max Yield" strategy. But more importantly, after reading it, you'll not only come away with a strategy for preserving your wealth in the face of an eroding dollar, you'll also learn a strategy for investing in the strongest and best-performing currencies in the world, year after year.

In fact, this strategy (The "Max Yield" strategy) can help you grow a $50,000 initial investment in cash into more than $220,000 almost 10 times faster than if you placed your capital into a super-safe one-year U.S. CD (at today's rates). Best of all, this strategy has averaged a double-digit return on cash for 35 years, and it has done so with all of the safety and security of having your money in the bank.

There's a perception in the world at large that there's eroding confidence in the U.S. dollar as a strong currency. This notion is often coupled with the view that the dollar's only backed by the Fed's ability to print money.

The Tale of Max Yield

In 1970, Max started out in the U.S. dollar. It was paying 10% at the time, and nothing was paying better.

So when January 1, 1971, rolled around, Max had $11,000. He saw that the German mark now offered 7.5% compared to the U.S.'s now 6%. So he converted to Deutsche marks and had DM40,000. A year later, with the 7.5% yield, Max had DM43,000. But it gets better, because during that year, the DM rose from approximately US$0.275 to US$0.31. So if converted back to dollars, Max's net worth was over $13,200 – for a 32% gain over a two-year period.

In January 1972, no yield was clearly higher than another. The Japanese yen was at 5.5% while the U.S. dollar and the German mark were at 5.375%. Not a big difference. But this may happen from time to time, so Max had to figure in the costs of transacting.

Should he switch out of the German DM into the yen or

the U.S. dollar? Because he thought the fees might be greater than the 0.125% difference, he stayed in German DM. And that was Max's first bad decision.

The German DM only rose 1% against the dollar while the yen rose 4% – depriving Max of 3%. So he resolved to always switch to the highest-paying rate, whatever it was.

In 1973, none of world's currencies could touch the English pound's rate of 9%. But this proved to be another stumbling block. By year's end, the pound's value had dropped to $2.22 against the dollar from its starting point of $2.36 – losing 6.8% of its value in dollar terms. That meant his 9% yield was now only a 2.2% gain.

Unfortunately, he would have made more in the U.S. dollar at 6%, and would have really scored had he remained in the German mark – as it rose 20% against the dollar from 31.3 cents to 37.6 cents. Now add in its 7.75% interest, and Max would have increased his pot by almost 28% for the year.

When 1974 began, Max found the pound paying a whopping 16%, so he stayed there. Sure enough, by the end of the year, the pound increased 4.7% against the dollar, and Max found himself with a 20.7% gain. The system was back on track.

In 1975, the only major currency even close to the pound's 1974 value of 16% was the Italian lira at 15.1%. But at the time, the lira wasn't quite a "respected" currency. So Max didn't bite. Instead, he got into the Japanese yen, which was paying a healthy 13.75%. That year, the yen lost 2% against the dollar, but Max still made an effective yield of 11.75%. So, during the first five years that Max worked his system, his $10,000 was up by 94%, with an average yield of 15.67% – all from keeping his money in the bank.

Not too bad.

The Roller Coaster Begins

Ironically, during the U.S.'s bicentennial year in 1976, the clear choice for Max was the British pound again. It paid 10% compared to 8.5% for the yen and 5.5% for the dollar. But the pound nose-dived that year, moving from $2.03 to $1.68 vs. the dollar (a 17.3% loss). For the first time since 1970, Max saw the interest earned completely wiped out, and his principal reduced by 7.3% when converted back to the dollar.

The following table shows how effective the "Max Yield" strategy has been from 1970 to 2005.

But in 1977, Max pressed on. And using the same system, the British pound was again the currency of choice, yielding 13.5%. The pound rose 10.5% that year on top of the yield for a 24% climb… the system's best ever.

In 1978, the only double-digit yield to be found was the Italian lira at 11%, but Max still couldn't trade lira very easily. So he opted for the next highest, the French franc at 9.25%. Good choice, as the franc rose by another 9.33% for a total return of almost 19% for the year.

So, after nine years of chasing yields, Max was sitting pretty. He'd made 160%, for an average of 18% annually. Plus, he'd had only one losing year.

That brought him to 1979… The pound was again at 12.5%. And when the switch across the channel (from the French franc to the British pound) led Max to a 10% profit on the pound soaring over the franc, he was in for a cool 22.5% that year. This made Max's 10-year take 223%.

The Soaring '80s?

The beginning of this decade saw the world's interest rates

spiraling upwards. Even the dollar was sporting a 14.33% yield. But again, the pound led the way at a hefty 17.33%. And again the pound rose, albeit only by 3.6%. Still, Max pocketed 20.95% for the year.

New Year's Day 1981 arrived, and a choice accompanied it.

The best yields were in "Eurodollar" deposits (U.S. dollars held in foreign banks) at 18%, but Canadian dollars were paying 17% and pounds 14.35%.

Max went with the foreign-held greenbacks and their 18%. Good thing too, as the pound fell 21% against the dollar that year. Max pocketed his 18%.

As 1982 began, the lira yielded an amazing 21.375%. The British pound 15.125%, and the dollar 14.25%. Finally, Max couldn't resist earning more than 20% in a bank account. And he paid for it (sort of) when the lira fell 13.9% against the dollar. Still, he "eked" out 7.5% on the yield.

Again in 1983, the lira was clearly the best choice, offering 19%. But that year proved even worse, as the lira swooned 21.3% against the dollar. This gave Max his second losing year in 14 for the system. But at this time, he also realized that for the third straight year, he would have been better off in the U.S. dollar itself. He wondered if his strategy had a flaw... But he preferred to not be swayed by these new facts and decided to stay the course.

In that most Orwellian of years, 1984, the pattern continued. There sat the lira taunting him with a fat 17.75% yield. The French franc was a distant second at 12.25% and the dollar a paltry (by comparison) 9.75%. Max chose the lira again, and once again the lira fell. This time by 14.75%, leaving him a small 3% gain. But the franc would have done worse, which was some consolation. But still, this was the fourth year in a row where the dollar outdistanced them all. And although Max's system began to look foolish, he stuck with it.

He hoped for better results in 1985. And that year, with the lira offering 15.7%, he got them. The lira gained 12.1% for a fabulous 27.8% in one year. Of course, the pound soared when it saw a 29.2% currency gain against the dollar on top of its 11.67% yield, for a whopping 40.9% return, but Max and others outside of the dollar were happy.

A Switch to Down Under Leaves Max Unsettled... But Not for Long

As 1986 arrived, Max looked upon the 1985 pound return of almost 41% with envy. And with the pound sitting at a "not-unattractive" 12.75% yield, it was tempting. But he steeled his resolve and pushed forward, going with something new: the Aussie dollar. It was paying 18.75%. Unfortunately, that year, the Aussie dollar lost 2.4%, but it still left Max with a 14.6% profit. But he felt a little bitter because, had he left his money in the lira for a fourth consecutive year, he would have seen a 35% profit (15% yield, plus 20% in the currency).

And 1987 again saw the Aussie dollar with the best rates (16% vs. 11.375% for the lira and 11% for the pound). And this time there was thunder Down Under, as the currency rose 8.7% for a total gain of 24.7%.

And 1988 saw more of the same. This year, the Aussie dollar led the way with a 12.875% yield, and the currency soared in value by 18.4%. Max realized a 31.3% gain. Perhaps more importantly, Max's original $10,000 investment jumped to more than $120,000 that year. So, in 19 years, his high-yield strategy was good for a profit of 1,100%, or an average annual yield of 58%.

The good news continued in 1989, as Aussie rates were still the best at 16.875%. And even though the currency dipped 7.3%, Max still earned 9.6%.

How Max Fared in the Early 1990s... 10 Grand into 58

And Max Yield stayed the course in 1990, as the Aussie dollar again led the way in yield with 15.75%. And even though the currency again fell (by only 2.2% this time), Max still profited by 13.55%.

By the time 1991 arrived, Max's account had grown to more than $150,000, a fantastic 1,4123% rise over 21 years. Had Max done like most Americans, and stayed at home with his money, his $10,000 investment would have been worth $58,000. Not bad, but almost tripling that was better.

That year, Max jumped hemispheres and landed in the Spanish peseta, with a yield of 14.49%. And even though the dollar rose against most currencies that year, the peseta only gave back 5.45%. So Max still made more than 9% – more than he would have gotten in the dollar.

Then, in 1992, Max had another choice: Should he roll his peseta T-bills – paying 12.21% – or should he look to still higher yields? The Swedish krona was then at 13.75% and the South African rand loomed above at 18.1%. South Africa had looked high for years, as the government had to pay up to lure investment. But now things were looking better. And Max remembered his Italian experience from a few years back, taking a gamble on a currency that was on the fringe.

Well, he ended up in the Swedish krona in 1992, and was greatly relieved when he saw the rand tank 26% against the dollar. The Swedish krona also fell, but only by 3%, so he'd still made more than 10%.

By the end of this first 21 years, Max had made 1,700% profits. His original $10,000 was now worth more than $182,000. Not too bad.

Max Yield and the Past Decade of Performance

As 1993 opened, he saw that Spain was yielding a fat 13.35%, so that was what Max chose. But at the same time, he became a member of an investment organization called *The Oxford Club*, which made a strong case for New Zealand. While this currency only paid 8%, *Oxford* pointed out that this country had gotten "its act together" in an extraordinary way, and deserved a vote of investor confidence.

He decided to follow *The Oxford Club's* advice with separate money. Well, the Spanish peseta in 1993 tumbled badly, by 23%. The hefty yield was not enough to forestall a 9.65% loss for the year. His hoard was down to $166,019.

But the advice that he had gotten in 1993 from *The Oxford Club* had proved extremely profitable. The New Zealand dollar rose by 10.13% that year, and adding the 8% yield, he made 18.13%, nearly enough to make up his peseta loss.

The Kiwi dollar was definitely on Max's radar screen. Interest rates the world over had fallen dramatically throughout 1993, and when 1994 rolled around, the best Max could find was, once again, the Spanish peseta, paying 7.73%. With misgivings, but still sticking to the plan, Max stayed put. But this time he was glad he did. The peseta rose, making a grand total return of 15.84%. He was back to a record $191,158.

Max had still held onto to his New Zealand dollars, which had continued to be quite profitable, so imagine his surprise when Jan. 1, 1995 arrived and he found that this very currency was paying the highest yield: the only double-digit yielder at 10.02%. So now his total holdings were switched to the Kiwi.

For the third year in a row, New Zealand paid off. The Kiwi dollar rose only 2.06% against the greenback, but that was enough to give a nice 12.08% total return, to $214,250.

In 1996 Max went "Italian" again, and again the system worked. Adding an 8.85% yield to a modest 3.5% currency gain, he totaled 12.35%, and had amassed $240,710.

In 1997 it was back to the Kiwi dollar. Though it paid 7.63%, that was the highest out there.

But 1997 was a fateful year for Asia. A lot of stock markets and currencies collapsed, and New Zealand was not immune. The Kiwi dollar plunged from 70.61 U.S. cents (much higher than it is even today) on January 1 to 58.35 cents (about where it is today). That was a fall of 17.36%. The 7.63% interest payment softened the blow somewhat to a loss of 9.73%, still steep and the worst Max had experienced for years. His total fell to $217,289.

As 1998 opened, Max stayed in the New Zealand dollar, as it still paid the most (8.40%). But again he was stung by the "Asian contagion." The Kiwi fell another 10.37%, to 52.30 U.S. cents. His total loss, cushioned by the hefty yields, was just 1.97%. But he was back at $213,008, about exactly where he had been three years earlier.

In 1999 Max was happy to wave goodbye to New Zealand and go to Great Britain. The pound paid a mere 5.63%, but it was still better than any other major currency. But it was becoming clear to Max that a U.S. dollar bull market was underway. For the third year in a row, his currency fell against the greenback. However, he still came out ahead, with a 3.12% total return, since sterling had fallen by just 2.51%. His "fund" had increased to $219,654.78.

Looking at what had been happening in the U.S. stock market as 2000 opened, Max wondered if he was on the right track with currencies. All his friends were bragging on Jan. 1 about how much they were making on the Nasdaq. Max was quiet: Better to be silent than to be thought a fool, he reasoned in a Lincoln-esque way.

He stayed put in the pound during 2000: It paid 6.71%, which seemed a pittance after he overheard one friend that day saying bitterly, "My broker only made me 15% last year, and I am ready to wring his neck!" Well, 2000 was to test Max again. The pound fell once more, this time by 7.74%, making a small total loss of 1.03%, sending his account to $217,392.

But when Jan. 1, 2001, came around his friends were not bragging so much about their stocks. Max discovered that they had lost far more than 1%. Max went back to New Zealand that year, and once again, for the fifth year in a row, the U.S. dollar triumphed.

The yield of 6.52% was not quite enough to cover the currency fall of 7.15%. The total loss was just 0.63%, but reduced Max's currency portfolio to $213,271.

The fact that his friends had lost even more in the stock markets in 2001 softened somewhat Max's doubts in the effectiveness of his system. After all, on Jan. 1, 2002, he had only about as much as he had six years earlier.

Would the dollar bull market ever end? Should he just throw in the towel and put it all back into dollars?

No. He stuck to his plan. "Hey," he thought, "at least I haven't really lost money, and I haven't suffered the catastrophes I'm hearing about from my stock-holding friends."

As 2002 opened, however, interest rates around the world were simply puny. The best, New Zealand again, paid a mere 4.84%.

But coincidentally, in early 2002 Max took a cruise around New Zealand on the Wind Star line. He stayed on a little while longer, and was amazed at how much his U.S. dollars bought. When the best hotel in Christchurch only cost US$40 per night, something was wrong.

The greenback was too high, and the kiwi too low. Bargains like this never last long. The Kiwi dollar was down around US$0.40.

Sure enough, the kiwi was too low. The NZ dollar soared over 2002 by 24.81%. Adding the interest yield, Max's fund rose 29.65%, vaulting to a massive $280,073. Were the good old days back?

On Jan. 1, 2003, Max was more than happy to stick to the New Zealand dollar. Even in the face of the massive currency rise, interest rates there had actually gone up (while in the U.S. over 2002 they had fallen to nearly nothing). He now got 5.76%.

Through the end of May, the New Zealand dollar had kept on rising, as a new U.S. dollar bear market now became clear to everyone. From its January 1, 2003 rate of US$0.5172, the NZ dollar rose to finish out 2003 at US$0.6545.

That is an increase of 26.54%. Add to this the 5.76% yield, and you got a total return of a whopping 32.3%. This brought Max's total amount from $280,073 to $370,537.26 – an increase of more than $90,000. Now keep in mind, some of this is just due to the magic of compound interest. But a lot is also due to the fantastic feeling of being in a currency that is soaring against the U.S. dollar.

At the start of the year, on January 1, 2004 the annual

interest rate was 5.48%. At the time, the NZ dollar again was US65.45 cents.

By the end of 2004, the NZ dollar stood at nearly US72.00 cents.

On currency alone, this equals an increase of 9.63%. The annualized 5.48% yield gives you a yield of about 5%. Add these two together for a total return, for 2004, of 14.63%. What had been worth $370,537.26 at the start of 2004 was worth $424,746.57 by the start of 2005.

In 2005, Max stayed with the New Zealand dollar again to collect its 6.45% return. Unfortunately the currency declined 4.94% over the course of the year, leavingMax with a return of 1.51% and a final value of $431,160.

The high yields on the Iceland krona drew Max into his seventh losing year. A 9.45% yield was offset by the currency's 10.66% decline. This small loss of 1.21% brought the account total to $425,943 at year-end.

But, 2007 turned out to be the best year yet for Max...or at least the most recent trade Max made. The Turkish lira offered a yield of 19.75% in 2007. Turkey's strengthening economy and a dismal year for the dollar drove a currency appreciation of 20.88%. Total returns were over 40% – the best year ever for the MaxYield strategy. After closing the position at year end, Max was left with $616,569 in his currency account.

And how did Max fare in 2008... during the worst financial crisis since the Great Depression? A lot better than you think.

Max decided once again that the Turkish lira was the place to be. Offering a 15.8% yield was too much to pass up. Alas, the U.S. dollar's unexpected surge wiped out his gains in the lira. It dropped 23.08% to give him a 7.28% loss for the year.

But when you consider the Dow lost 34%, its worst year since 1931, a 7.28% looks downright rosy. Most traders would be outright bragging about a loss as small as Max's.

And since beginning his experiment, and despite the financial crisis of 2008, Max had turned just $10,000 into $639,612.09 – a total return of 6,296%.

Even better, he had not suffered through any crashes like his stock market friends had. The worst that had happened were temporary plateaus.

And even including dividends, there is no way that staying in the stock market since 1970 has bettered MaxYield's simple strategy.

The following table shows how effective the "MaxYield" strategy has been over the last 40 years.

MAX YIELD INTEREST CURRENCY INCREASE TOTAL

Year	Max Yield Currency	Interest Paid	Currency Value	Increase Total Returns US$	
1970	US$	10.000%	NA	$11,000.00	
1971	German DM	7.500%	16.000%	$13,200.00	
1972	German DM	5.500%	1.000%	$14,058.00	
1973	British Pound	9.000%	-6.800%	$14,367.28	
1974	British Pound	16.000%	4.700%	$17,341.30	
1975	Japenese Yen	13.750%	-2.000%	$19,378.91	
1976	British Pound	10.000%	-17.300%	$17,964.25	1st Losing Year
1977	British Pound	13.500%	10.500%	$22,275.66	
1978	French franc	9.250%	9.330%	$26,414.48	
1979	British Pound	12.500%	10.000%	$32,357.74	
1980	British Pound	17.330%	3.600%	$39,130.22	
1981	Eurodollars	18.000%	0.000%	$46,173.65	
1982	Italian lira	21.375%	-13.900%	$49,625.14	
1983	Italian lira	19.000%	-21.300%	$48,483.76	2nd Losing Year
1984	Italian lira	17.750%	-14.750%	$49,938.27	
1985	Italian lira	15.700%	12.100%	$63,821.11	
1986	Australian dollar	18.750%	-2.400%	$74,255.86	
1987	Australian dollar	16.000%	8.700%	$92,597.06	

1988	Australian dollar	12.875%	18.400%	$121,556.79	
1989	Australian dollar	16.875%	-7.300%	$133,195.85	
1990	Australian dollar	15.750%	-2.200%	$151,243.89	
1991	Spanish peseta	14.490%	-5.450%	$164,916.34	
1992	Swedish krone	13.750%	-3.000%	$182,644.84	
1993	Spanish peseta	13.350%	-23.000%	$165,019.61	
1994	Spanish peseta	7.730%	8.110%	$191,158.72	
1995	NZ dollar	10.020%	2.060%	$214,250.69	
1996	Italian lira	8.850%	3.500%	$240,710.66	
1997	NZ dollar	7.630%	-17.360%	$217,289.51	3rd Losing Year
1998	NZ dollar	8.400%	-10.370%	$213,008.91	4th Losing Year
1999	British Pound	5.630%	-2.510%	$219,654.78	
2000	British Pound	6.710%	-7.740%	$217,392.34	5th Losing Year
2001	New Zealand	6.520%	-7.150%	$216,022.77	6th Losing Year
2002	NZ dollar	4.840%	24.810%	$280,073.52	
2003	NZ dollar	5.760%	26.54%	$370,537.26	
2004	NZ dollar	5.00%	9.630%	$424,746.57	
2005	NZ dollar	6.450%	-4.940%	$431,160.54	
2006	Iceland krona	9.450%	-10.660%	$425,943.50	7th Losing Year
2007	Turkish lira	19.750%	20.880%	$616,569.40	
2008	Turkish lira	15.800%	-23.08%	$553,824.83	8th Losing Year
2009	Turkish lira	14.50%	0.99%	$639,612.29	

*NZ = New Zealand dollar

Action to Take: *Contact one of the recommended brokers listed below to begin your own Max Yield program.*

Editor's Note: Chris Weber is the editor of *The Weber Global Opportunities Report* and the inventor of the "Max-Yield Strategy," which has averaged double-digit returns every year for the past 30 years. You can read a detailed account about Chris and his investment successes and get more information on how to subscribe to *The Weber Global Opportunities Report* by visiting www.weberglobal.net

Aden Research
Dept SJO 874, PO Box 025216
Miami, FL 33102-5216
weberglobal@racsa.co.cr | 866.301.2933

For investors who would like to put Max Yield's strategy to work in your portfolios, in the United States, Chris Weber refers you to:

Jeff Winn Chris Gaffney
International Assets EverBank
300 South Orange Ave., Suite 1100 1610 Des Peres Road, Suite 130
Orlando, FL 32801 St Louis, MO 63131
Tel: 800.432.4402 or 407.254.1522 Tel: 800.926.4922 or 314.984.0892
Fax: 407.254.1505 Fax: 888.882.0073 or
E-mail:jwinn@iaac.com 314.984.0875
www.everbank.com

For offshore investing, you can contact:

Camafin Trust in Zurich
Landstrasse 147
8800 Thalwill-Zurich
SWITZERLAND
Account Minimum: US$100,000
Contact: Roger Badet
Tel: 41.1.720.3131 Fax: 41.1.720.3141

Jyske Bank
Thomas Fischer
yske Bank Private Banking
Vesterbrogade 9
DK-1780 Copenhagen V
DENMARK
Account Minimum: $14,000 Euro or approx.
Tel: 45.3.378.7812 Fax: 45.3.378.7833 E-mail:
Fischer@Jyskebank.dk

Anglo Irish Bank of Vienna
Rathaustrasse 20

P.O. Box 306
A-1011 Vienna
AUSTRIA
Account Minimum: US$25,000
Contact: Mr. Patrick Doherty
Tel: 43.1.406.6161 Fax: 43.1.405.8142 E-mail:
welcome.desk@angloirishbank.at

Jyske Bank Private Banking
Wasserwekstrasse 12 Postfach
CH-8035 Zurich
SWITZERLAND
Minimum Investment SF100,000
Tel: 41.1.368.7351 or 41.1.368.7373 Fax: 41.1.368.7379 |
www.jpbp.com
E-mail: jyskebank@jyskebank.ch or
kimnielsen@jyskebank.ch

BUC Bank of Geneva
3, Rue de Monte Blanc
CH-1211 Geneva
SWITZERLAND
E-mail: ursfrei@buc.ch

Pictet Bank
Bd Georges-Favon 29 Geneva
SWITZERLAND
E-mail: www.pictet.com

Note: *The Oxford Club* is not a broker, dealer or licensed investment advisor. No person listed below should be considered as permitted to engage in personalized investment advice as an agent of *The Oxford Club*. *The Oxford Club* does not receive any compensation for these services. Additionally, any individual services rendered to *The Oxford Club* members by the members of the Advisory Panel are considered completely separate from and outside the scope of services offered by *The Oxford Club*. Therefore if you choose to contact a member of the Advisory Panel, such contact, as well as any resulting relationship is strictly between you and the Panel member.

KEITH FITZ-GERALD
The Only Emerging Market Worth Talking About: China is Gunning for the U.S.

As the old Avis rental car slogan used to say: "When you're No. 2, you try harder."

With the growth rates that its economy has turned in the past few years, no economist could ever accuse China's leader of not trying hard. China now claims to have jumped over Japan to take over the No. 2 spot in the world economic pecking order.

China's next target: The No. 1 U.S. economy.

In fact, some experts believe that China could catch up to the United States' $14.4 trillion economy in as little as 10 to 15 years.

The stark, inescapable reality for those who would dismiss China is that China's growth is not only very real, but has the greatest upside potential in recorded history.

Yi Gang, the country's chief currency regulator and director of the State Administration on Foreign Exchange, said that China has achieved the No. 2 spot during an interview in *China Reform* magazine. China came close to surpassing Japan in 2009 and has continued its torrid economic growth ever since.

China's $4.81 trillion economy is still growing rapidly despite its size. This year gross domestic product (GDP) growth is averaging 11.1% so far and will likely end the year with double-digit growth. GDP is expected to grow at a better-than 9% clip next year. China's annual growth since its market reforms of 1978 has averaged more than 9.5%.

Yi said that although the country will not be able to keep up a robust growth rate of 9% – 10% each decade, if China can maintain a rate of at least 5% – 6% through the 2020s, it would reach 50 straight years of rapid growth – what he calls

---

WHEN YOU'RE NO. 2, YOU TRY HARDER...

Mainland China has surpassed Japan to become the world's No. 2 economy.

The United States is next.

Goldman Sachs Group Inc., the World Bank and others believe that – even with a bit of slowdown – the Red Dragon could overtake the United States and its economy (currently $14.4 trillion) to become the world's largest by 2025. Money Morning Chief Investment Strategist Keith Fitz-Gerald says it could happen even sooner – by 2020.

The numbers bear this out.

According to CIA Factbook, China's per-capita gross domestic product (GDP) was $3,619 for 2009 (based on official exchange rate GDP vs. GDP purchasing power parity) – giving it a total estimated GDP of $4.81 trillion. The United States' comparable per capita GDP for last year was $46,513 – giving it a total GDP of $14.43 trillion.

Here's where our research shows us that it gets interesting.

Consider that, when China achieves a per-capita GDP of:

- $8,000, the country's GDP will be $10.64 trillion.
- $10,000, the country's GDP will be $13.30 trillion.
- and $12,000, the country's GDP will be $15.96 trillion.

At 8% GDP growth, China will surpass the (current) U.S. economy by 2025, when its per-capita GDP is only $10,900. When China is able to increase its per-capita GDP to $15,504 (one-third of the current U.S figure), its economy will be $20.622 trillion – or about 40% larger than the U.S. economy is right now.

Sources: CIA Factbook, Money Morning staff research

"unprecedented in human history." Its current 30-year climb has helped it surpass the economies of Britain and France in 2005 and Germany in 2007.

Where China still lags behind its closest economic competition is in the area of per-capita income. With a World Bank ranking of 124, China comes in at $3,800 a year, which is a far cry from Japan, which is ranked No. 32 at $37,870, and the United States, ranked No. 17 at $46,513.

By maintaining an average annual GDP growth rate of 8%, China could overtake the U.S. economy by 2025 – with a per capita GDP that's less than one-third the comparable U.S. number.

China could snag the top spot even earlier – maybe as soon as 2020 – less than 10 years from now.

"There's no doubt there's going to be ups and downs, and there's going to be bubbles and growth spurts, just like we've experienced in our own economies, but data like this suggests that it's just par for the course," Fitz-Gerald said.

China's poor water quality and immature financial markets are the only impediments to its growth, but having a limited variety of financial instruments has also been a positive factor for China.

It means China has not engaged in the nonsense that drove the rest of the world to financial oblivion.

Skeptics who think China's communist environment will impede its financial strength simply aren't looking at all the facts.

Where is it written that you have to be democratic to be capitalist – except in our own book? The China of the future is likely to include a blend of capitalism, communism and democratic principles that are in their infancy today.

Although China has gained political clout with its increasingly powerful financial position, Yi said that the country's No. 2 spot did not mean it was eager to make the yuan a global currency soon.

"China is still a developing country, and we should be wise enough to know ourselves," Yi said. "We must be modest and we still have to keep a low profile. If other people choose the yuan as a reserve currency, we won't stop that, as it is the demand of the market. However, we will not push hard to promote it."

China's increased ranking gives yet another reason for investors to ensure they are part of a market offering historic profit opportunities. Investors should consider doubling their exposure to China.

The dragon is coming to lunch. The only decision investors have to make is whether you will be at the table or on the menu.

JUSTIN FORD
Teach Your Kids Millionaire Habits With the Priceless Two-Box System

Oxford Club Investment Director Alex Green hopes his kids grow up with a good savings ethic and a good work ethic. But honestly, he didn't have a real plan to get them there... until he read about **Justin Ford's** Two-Box System...

He liked the idea so much, he wanted to try it in his own household. If you've got kids or grandkids, you ought to consider it too...

It's brilliant. And it's easy. Sometimes you may feel like you've heard it all in the investment business. But every once in a while, an ingenious idea comes along.

Justin has written a program called "Seeds of Wealth" to get your children (or grandchildren) off on the right path to wealth.

One part of his program is the "Two-Box System." By using this "Two-Box System," you can assure that your children not only learn the fundamentals of wealth building at a very early age – they'll actually become wealthy at a relatively early age.

We find the "Two-Box System" to be so valuable that we've asked Justin to share the basics of it with us, along with how it has worked in his household. Here's what he had to say...

Your Child's Most Powerful "Investment" Weapon: The Two-Box System Explained

"Kids, how would you each like a million dollars?"

Try that at the dinner table. It's a guaranteed attention-getter...

So exactly how do you start your child on his or her "march to millions?" Strangely enough, it all begins with two ordinary shoeboxes – one marked "permanent savings," the other marked "money for spending." It works like this...

Every time your child gets money – whether it's allowance from you, birthday money from the grandparents, or cash from doing odd jobs around the house or in the neighborhood – half of it goes into one box... and half into the other.

The spending box contains money your child can spend on anything he or she wants – toys, candy, movies and popcorn... anything you allow. The savings box is money your child can never touch – money that will find its way to safe, long-term investments that, over time, will grow into hundreds of thousands – even millions – of dollars.

It Really Works... There's Proof!

From Alex's own experience, he can tell you the Two-Box System is not a great sacrifice for kids. On the contrary, the habits this simple technique helps instill should help your children enjoy what they do have all the more without becoming spoiled, or contracting the dreaded "Gimme Disease."

His youngest child, for instance, has known exactly how much of each dollar must be put into the "permanent savings" box on his dresser and how much goes into his "temporary savings" box ever since he was five. He counts out his permanent savings twice a year, and Alex invests it for him. He can spend all or part of his temporary savings on whatever he wants.

Together, they've counted out hundreds of dollars from his permanent savings box in the last year alone. And that means he's also had a few hundred dollars to spend. So it's really no sacrifice at all. After all, what could a nine-year-old gain by spending a few hundred extra dollars? And he's developing habits now where he wouldn't *dream* of spending all of his money!

And the same goes with Alex's oldest child. When she won $50 and a pen for first prize in an essay contest, she kept the pen and immediately divided the money between the two boxes – just as she's been doing for years. She splits her allowance and household-chore money the same way.

Alex also got his nephew to try the two-box system. He's a teenager and no longer receives an allowance, yet every two weeks, he mows the lawn and his aunt's lawn. He automatically puts half his yard-work earnings into his permanent savings and spends the other half as he pleases. He does the same with money he receives from birthday or Christmas presents, and he'll do the same with money he'll earn when he takes his first part-time job.

These habits are now second nature to all three of these children. They actually have better money habits than Justin did when he was a youngster… And that was the whole point of writing Seeds of Wealth. To establish the fundamentals of wealth building early in life.

But What Happens When the Kids Grow Up?

As the creator of *Seeds of Wealth*, Justin Ford teaches parents and grandparents specific techniques for helping kids develop lifelong wealth-building habits. Every once in a while a parent will write and ask, "But what happens when my children come of legal age? They gain control over their investment accounts, so what's to prevent them from squandering the wealth they've accumulated?"

The primary answer to this question is that the program is really about developing responsible financial habits for their lifetimes, not just growing wealth at a young age. They'll have created wealth themselves through their own discipline. So they'll know wealth is not an easy-come proposition and are less likely to have an easy-go attitude about it. In other words, their very financial character has been molded from the beginning, so going on a spending spree would feel "unnatural" to them.

Don't forget the intangible benefits: **Your kids will never have to worry about not having enough money in their lives – no matter what careers they choose**. They'll have more options professionally, in terms of travel and education. And from a very young age, they'll learn from experience the kinds of things they can achieve with a little discipline. They'll gain wealth and have a good savings and work ethic. And they'll have you to thank for it.

JOHN BOGLE
Four Key Elements of Investing and the Three You Can Actually Control

"*The one great secret of investment success is that there is no secret.*" – **JOHN BOGLE**, FOUNDER OF VANGUARD FUNDS

Alex Green frequently speaks at investment conferences around the country. At the conferences, attendees have the opportunity to hear the investment "secrets" of probably over 25 presenters. When you think about it, that's enough to make anyone's head spin... Imagine if each "guru" gives five secrets and three stock tips. That's 200 pieces of advice that you've got to consider using when you get home. We wonder if after all of that advice, attendees aren't worse off... instead of better off.

The Most Important Secret of All...

It may sound pompous of us, but we don't know how else to put this. We've got the most important secret to share of all...

Out of all 200 pieces of expert advice, what we are about to share with you will probably improve the most lives 10 years from now, and ruin the least. Because the one thing that we're going to share is **John Bogle's** one great secret of investment success "*that there is no secret.*"

Everybody knows this, we think. Or at least, deep down, they understand the concept that there's no free lunch. But for the same reasons people head to Vegas, people head here. Quite frankly, they're looking to get lucky – to get the 100%-plus winner.

Let's consider the fate of two folks 15 years from now – one looking for luck and the other one accepting that there is no secret about a sound investment plan. If both guys start with $100,000, we'd wager that the guy looking for the lucky 100% winner would have less than he started with in 15 years time, if he hadn't inadvertently lost it all in the process.

Meanwhile, the guy who invested and earned a fairly unsexy 10% a year would likely end up with about $450,000. John Bogle's secret – "that there is no secret" – is big. As soon as you accept it, you won't be snowed by "get rich quick" schemes ever again. When you get that "Turn $2,000 into $2 million in 2 years" pitch, you'll look for the holes. And by doing this, you'll be on your way to generating wealth the only way that we know can truly work.

John Bogle has 50-plus years of professional investing behind him. He woke up every day, and spent his whole day considering the craft of investing. After 50 years, he should know what he's talking about.

There Is No Substitute for Real World Experience

Steve has achieved as much as you can, education-wise. And he stays informed, literally crunching tens of thousands of data points on Tuesday across 50 spreadsheets as part of his usual research. And he can tell you that, while this is good, this is not enough to make you a great investor. The truth is, you need real world experience.

At the New Orleans Conference, there are lots of Wall Street pros... Having been a hedge-fund manager, having headed research departments, having been a broker, an institutional trader and more, Steve's got the Wall Street experience as well. But he knows even that isn't enough. You've got to pound the pavement as well.

He's visited companies from the top of the world to the

bottom of the world looking for investments. And he's probably stood on more stock exchange floors than most. He's visited companies in Iceland like Ossur (www.ossur.com) and Decode Genetics (www.decode.com), and bought bonds there as well. And he's visited companies at the bottom of the world in Argentina, including oil & gas and a real estate firm (NYSE: IRS). He's stood on stock exchange floors in Shanghai (where the traders were sleeping) and met with Central Bankers in Budapest. All in the name of finding winners.

He can say this to prove beyond a shadow of a doubt that he's seen it all – he's been there, done that..

He's done more homework than you might have a chance to. And he can tell you that John Bogle is right... "that there is no secret."

So – now that we've established that there is no magic "secret" – where do we go from here?

The Four Key Elements of Investing

Here's what you need to know. In essence, there are four key elements to investing:

1. **Risk**
2. **Reward**
3. **Time**
4. **Cost**

In general, most investors only consider **reward** in making their investment decisions. It's funny then, that this is the only element that is completely out of our control... yet it's the one we focus on. Go figure.

For example, nobody knows if the Nasdaq will go to 5,000 or 500 next year. Yet it's all people talk about. If we accept "that there is no secret," than we can go about making money much more systematically. That's because we **can** control the other three elements to investing...

What We Can Control as Investors

For example, we can control the element of **time** in our investments. We decide when we buy and when we sell a stock.

Are we short-term speculators? Or long-term investors? That is in our control. When we start saving and when we start taking the money out, those are choices we make as well.

We can control **cost**. If you buy a mutual fund from a broker, you may pay a 4% sales charge and a total of 2% a year in fees, for a total of 6% in fees in the first year. On the other hand, if you buy an index fund from Vanguard, you'll pay closer to 0.2%. That's an extraordinary difference – especially when you consider that 6% a year is all Warren Buffett and Bill Gross expect stocks to return over this decade.

If you accept that "*that there is no secret*," then why would you eat up your entire first year return, and a full one-third of future year returns, in costs when you don't have to. You've got to control your costs. And you can. And this doesn't even require much homework.

We can control how much **risk** we take. We can choose to take no risk and stick our money under a mattress. We can choose to take extraordinary risks and trade some fancy options strategy. And we can choose everything in between. If we're smart, we'll choose to lower our risk by spreading out our assets across different investment categories (stocks, bonds, real estate, cash, etc.), thereby reducing our overall exposure to any one asset, and reducing our risk. We can control our risk.

The quicker you accept the greatest secret – "that there is

no secret" – the quicker you'll be on the proven path to generating wealth. And the smartest way to follow that path is to concentrate on the three elements of investing that you can control, not the one that is completely out of your control.

The Oxford Club Recommended Reading List

11 CHEAP RESOURCES GUARANTEED TO HELP YOU BECOME A BETTER INVESTOR

We're often asked what resources we check every day to stay on top of the markets... as there's so much *information* out there... and yet, so little *knowledge*.

So, we'll share what the *Oxford Club* team – founder and publisher, **Julia Guth**; Chairman, **Alexander Green**; Publisher **Alex Williams** and Advisory Panelists **Dr. Mark Skousen** and **Dr. Scott Brown** – read in the office every day and every week (the non-book stuff, in other words) so we don't miss a thing...

On a daily basis, nothing beats the *Financial Times* (www.ft.com) – the peach-colored newspaper out of London.

You know what's going on in news, business and investing from an international perspective. We also thumb through *The Wall Street Journal* (www.wsj.com) and read a few stories. As an individual investor, if you can read both of these at least once a week, you'll have a huge advantage over the investing herd...

Or you could just read these weeklies... On a weekly basis, *The Economist* magazine (www.economist.com) is exceptional when it comes to knowing what's going on in the world. For investments, we flip the pages of *Barron's* (www.barrons.com), mostly enjoying the interviews. On a monthly basis, we generally thumb through *Fortune* (www.Fortune.com) and *Forbes* (www.Forbes.com).

We don't read that many newsletters in our office, believe it or not. And the ones we read are not the ones you might expect...

Popular letters in our office are **Richard Russell's** *Dow Theory Letters* (www.dowtheoryletters.com) and **Marc Faber's** *Gloom, Boom, and Doom Report* (www.gloomboomdoom.com). We don't really read these for the advice... but more for the long-range perspective. These are not essential for you.

One daily letter that is particularly useful is *The Gartman Letter*. Anyone trading in the short-term without it is trading at a severe disadvantage. Dennis Gartman somehow is able to deliver a full newsletter to our e-mail inbox every day around 5:30 in the morning... with tidbits and insights that very few are reporting on. It's not cheap... but if you're trading in size, it's worth it.

For tracking your stocks and for following the news on them, *Yahoo!* does a great job for free. The guys in our office use it (http://finance.yahoo.com).

For tracking our trailing stops in the office, we use XLQplus, which you can try for free for 45 days (www.qmatix.com). For daily information and news on gold and precious metals, use *Kitco* (www.kitco.com).

That should be plenty to keep you busy. And (with the exception of the newsletters), these things won't cost you an arm and a leg... most of it is probably available for free at your local library... Now you know what *The Oxford Club* team looks at every day to stay on top of the markets.

By sticking with the information-resources above, you'll be focused on the best research and writing out there. You won't waste your time reading things that aren't useful, or worse, things that could lose you money.

RICK RULE
Make Big Money Betting Against the Crowd: Our Interview With the Ultimate Contrarian

With uncertainty on the rise, it's a great time to seek wisdom from one of the most successful contrarian investors' we know; Rick Rule, President of **Global Resource Investments**. Rick's a trusted natural resource expert and long-time friend of *The Oxford Club*. He's helped members make substantial returns on his hedge funds for years. *Club* founder Bill Bonner calls Rick "probably the best hedge fund manager of the past decade."

Sometimes Rick is a bit early on his contrarian picks, like he was with uranium, but we like that he's way ahead of the game. Needless to say, when Rick talks... we listen.

Oxford Club: **As you know Rick,** *The Oxford Club* **takes a globally oriented, opportunistic approach to investing. We're not "gloom and doom" or eternally bullish either. We're market neutral… but always fully invested with an asset allocation that includes stocks in sectors we think have the most momentum.**

Your approach is a little different than ours in that you focus on one investment sector – natural resources. However, we know that you also take an opportunistic approach within that sector because it is extremely broad and the best opportunities are constantly shifting. You're also a globally oriented investor and have earned a reputation for finding very profitable investments in some far corners of the globe. Can you elaborate a little more on your focus?

Rick Rule: My firm, Global Resource Investments, is often thought of as specializing in junior mining stocks. And although we've certainly done a lot of work there, I would describe our focus as much more broadly based in natural resources. We are very interested in agriculture, water resources and alternative energy: The whole panoply, really.

My own belief is that, right now, the junior mining stock market is substantially ahead of itself and higher priced than the underlying valuation justifies. So lately, we have been more involved in selling rather than buying. We have a long-term focus on the industry, as it has treated us very well. And we will be, in some fashion, involved in the industry certainly until I am dead.

OC: What is your criteria?

RR: VALUE! In a very high-risk, high-reward business, most of our competition chases reward. We try to manage risk. It is our belief that, in high-risk and high-reward businesses, if you manage risk... the reward will take care of itself.

The basic blueprint that I follow is to look for companies that provide me with the highest comfort level. In a nutshell, what I'm looking for is:

- Value. If a company has a $50 million market capitalization, what's the underlying value that makes it worth $50 million? The fact that the stock gets lucky and goes higher isn't enough. We look for intrinsic value.

- The second thing we look for, on par with the first criteria, are the people involved: **Management**. Who are the key players involved with the company? I want experienced people with a track record of success at the top.

- Thirdly, we are looking for **High Quality Assets or Properties**. How geologically credible is the deposit and how will the economic value of the resource be unlocked?

Of course, there is a lot more research that goes into it... but at the core, I would define the metrics of our success as being attraction to value, attraction to top-quality people and attraction to companies that are trying to do something significant enough that a success will matter. And for me, that means being in the right sector at the right time in the business cycle. Many people attempt to find small mines that – with a little luck – occasionally succeed. But a small mine will never make you big money, though it does expose you to big and often unnecessary risk.

OC: How about strategy? Do you have any particular words of wisdom on how to play the market?

RR: The most important thing to grasp in my investment universe is that natural resource-based businesses are extremely cyclical and extremely volatile. What that means is that the only strategy that works over time is a contrarian strategy, albeit one anchored in logic. It is my belief that in the natural resource-based businesses, *you are either a contrarian or a victim.*

When all of your competition is terrified to be in the market, valuations are very cheap and you need to be very aggressive. You must have strong convictions in your philosophy and application thereof. When everybody collec-tively is feeling very smart and the sector is going to the moon, it is time to reduce your exposure and grab cash for the down cycle. Once again, sticking to your convictions based on logic... not emotion.

So I would say my strategy is simple: Understand the business cycle and be a logic-based contrarian. My contrarian approach has always helped me find my biggest winners. At times, I have certainly had to wait longer than I anticipated for my convictions to bear fruit... but this strategy has consistently, over many years, been successful for me.

OC: In your opinion, why does a contrarian strategy continue to work, year-after-year?

RR: What happens is that an investment that performs well causes people to understand the reasons for its performance. And the very performance of the investment validates the thesis and thus becomes a self-reinforcing prophecy, to the point whereby people pay for a story that has already proven itself. They bid it up to a level that can't be sustained. And it works the same way on the negative side... an investment gets bashed to a level that is well below what it's intrinsically worth. Market factors inevitably push investments to extremes. My personal experience tells me that to be successful, I need to discipline myself to be a contrarian and to do fewer transactions. I concentrate my efforts on people who have proven themselves to me in the past.

OC: Rick, let's diverge for a minute and talk about some of today's top investment topics. Please give us your thoughts on the U.S. dollar.

RR: The U.S. dollar is a terrible currency – unfortunately, so are all the others. And while foreign investors don't trust the United States or the U.S. dollar, they mostly don't trust other countries, either. The U.S. $13 trillion debt is a few zeros past my level of comprehension. But while the situation is hopeless... it doesn't have to be serious. There is no reason we as investors have to participate in the stupidity. I personally like the idea of having a passport from one country, assets in another and residency in yet another. Easier said than done and probably not practical advice for most, however, everyone can – and should – have investments outside of the U.S. dollar.

OC: Gold is a hot commodity and a hot topic right now. In your estimation, where are we in the gold cycle?

RR: Gold is performing very well. Previous to this bullish run, it has been a while since it has warranted any notice. So in the broader investment community, the luster has been off gold for some period of time.

But I think you are seeing more and more of the larger financial institutions coming to the point of view that the big store of value, the U.S. dollar, doesn't store value very well. I think you are seeing increasing attention being paid in circles outside of our own in the gold business. So, although gold has moved up nicely... I'm a believer that it still has much further to go. But be careful and tighten up your trailing stops along the way.

OC: Can you explain why gold and silver are money metals and not merely commodities?

RR: Gold and silver are well suited to be money. Each has value in and of itself, they are divisible and they are durable. Speaking of gold, of particular importance for me is an asset that isn't simultaneously someone else's liability. A dollar bill conveys for me the right to draw, at least on faith, but it is someone else's liability. If you have an ounce of gold, nobody owes you anything. You have it; it's physically there. And it can't be debased. Those are all very important reasons.

But maybe more importantly, gold and silver act as money because they ARE money. Over time, in civilizations that were varied both by geography and time, gold and silver have functioned as money on every continent. And they continue to do so to this very day. We are probably at a place – at least in modern history – where we have the least amount of market share by way of gold and silver as currency.

But my suspicion is that will change. I think people will be tired of being short-changed by the collective. Maybe not in five years, maybe not in 10 years. But I don't see people accepting it as a medium of exchange – a bank note, considering it's an asset that's simultaneously somebody else's liability. I am less comfortable accepting them.

OC: What words of caution would you give to investors considering junior gold and silver stocks?

RR: Just because gold and silver prices are moving up doesn't mean you can randomly invest in juniors and anticipate that the rising tide will lift all ships. Most juniors are doomed. Ninety-five percent of the sector has no value. Going back to the three absolute basic essentials I mentioned earlier, the vast majority of juniors don't even have these three characteristics... In fact, many don't have a single high-quality criteria going for them.

I don't think I can be clearer than that. I think the sector as a whole is toxic. I think investors need to be very careful here. Only 5% of the companies are investment worthy; the rest are paper business plans with little to no investment merit.

OC: Wow. You certainly didn't sugar coat that assessment. You sound like you're trying to scare investors away from the sector.

RR: Well, having said that... I love the natural resource sector and the junior mining industry. In my mind, it's absolutely the best place to find "diamonds in the rough." It's been very, very good to me. I've made a comfortable living for myself and helped make many clients a lot wealthier also. But there will always be circumstances where you have a liar standing next to a hole in the ground calling it a "goldmine"... and it's important to be able to recognize these situations.

OC: Rick, can you give our readers some insight into what your best contrarian investment sector is right now?

RR: There are several contrarian themes I am following

right now. I like agriculture and agricultural supplies, like equipment and fertilizer. If agriculture prices go up, that will favor the companies that provide the "picks and shovels." This sector is a long-term investment... one where boredom will trump terror. Agriculture will do well because, as small capital wealth increases in emerging markets, it will result in higher caloric diets in those countries.

When it comes to alternative energy, I continue to favor geothermal and hydro, not solar and wind. Why not invest in a business where the company has low capital costs around 4%? Yet,you can get utility-like returns of 15%.

OC: Thanks so much Rick. Always a pleasure!